# KITES

by
WYATT BRUMMITT

Illustrated by
ENID KOTSCHNIG

**GOLDEN PRESS • NEW YORK**
Western Publishing Company, Inc.
Racine, Wisconsin

W9-BEC-283

# FOREWORD

You can be as scientific about kites as you please. Experiment with them...theorize about them...but enjoy them. They are fun to design, fun to build, and fun to fly.

Kite flying today is not the same as kiting only a few years ago. Many of the kites are different, the equipment is far better, and the techniques of flying have changed. There's no frantic running to get a kite air-borne. A well-behaved modern kite takes off from your hand and, assuming reasonable skill and luck, returns obediently to your hand.

A kite that leaps from your hand, making do with the erratic ground winds until it reaches the level of the real wind, is a joy. With your help it finds its natural, most comfortable flying angle, then climbs and climbs. Even when it becomes a speck, far up and away, it needs only a twitch on the line to be reminded that you are its master.

When it comes time to bring it down, the modern kite doesn't scatter itself all over the sky. It obeys as you slack off to let it fall, reel in, slack off, reel in...until, at last, there it is, just above you. You reach up, catch the bridle— and your bird is safely, successfully home.

This book never strays very far from the idea that kites are fun—for anyone, at any age. And the more you improvise on kites, kite designs, kite-flying techniques, and kite hunches, the greater your fun will be.

W. B.

# CONTENTS

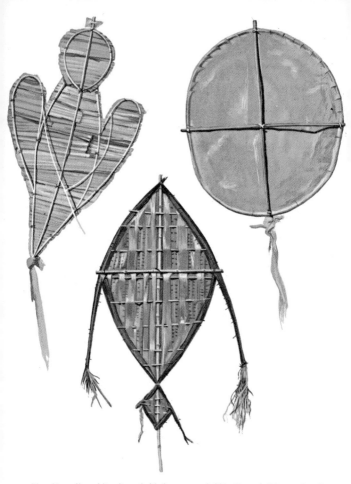

The Hawaiian kite (top left) is made of banana leaves stretched over a frame. It is similar in construction to very primitive kites. Also Hawaiian is the round kite (top right), made of paper. The fish-shaped kite (bottom) consists of thin, woven strips of bamboo over a bamboo frame.

4

# THE HISTORY OF KITES

Kites were used in Malayan religious observances 3,000 years ago. Legends about tethered flight can be read in 2,500-year-old Egyptian hieroglyphics. Assuming that kites had been known for a long time before they became a part of legend, folklore, or religion, it seems reasonable to believe that kites date to the beginnings of human cultures. China may well have been their birthplace.

The earliest kites were probably large leaves of semi-tropical plants flown from lines made of twisted vines. Certainly natural forms and materials would have been used before fabrications. Given a salubrious climate, luxurious vegetation, and steady breezes, it is easy to dream up a bemused Oriental observing the miracle of a big leaf supported in the air at the end of a long stem. This, obviously, was magic. Things did not naturally float in the air; they dropped to the ground.

We do not know how long it took our observant Oriental, or generations of his descendants, to determine that some leaves flew or floated better than others or to discover that the tether could be lengthened or varied in size to improve the flight. It was probably many centuries before man made his own "flying leaf" of skin drawn tight over a bamboo frame or of woven reeds. And when he finally achieved something that climbed into the heavens, it was inescapably religious. It linked man and the heavens. Malayan priests deemed it a sacred duty to protect their ceremonial kites from the prying eyes of curious foreigners.

Even today, in our matter-of-fact culture, there is something just a little beyond simple fun in the way a kite extends your hand's reach into the sky.

# IN ANCIENT CHINA

During the Han Dynasty, which bracketed the beginnings of the Christian era, kites were used by Huan Theng, staff scholar-advisor to the Emperor, to demoralize an invading barbarian army. He had a number of kites built with a bamboo pipe or hummer in each. On a dark, windy night he flew the kites over the encamped besiegers. The wailing and moaning from the black sky unnerved the enemy. Huan Theng followed through by infiltrating spies who spread the word that the mysterious sounds were the voices of the gods proclaiming the doom of the invaders. With this, so the legend goes, the invaders panicked and fled.

About 500 A.D., the Emperor Liang Moo put kites to work as military signals. Keeping his army on constant alert in the palace compound was not practical, so he arranged for his farmer-soldiers to continue their work in the nearby fields until they saw kites fly high above the palace. The kites, visible air-raid sirens, brought the defenders on the double.

In pre-Mao China, every September 9 was a kite-flying holiday, the Festival of Ascending on High. Traditionally, kites were symbols of good luck and of the soaring aspirations of the human soul. So on that day, the skies were crowded with elaborately decorated kites with the most elegant of tails. Most spectacular were huge dragon kites, so big that teams of men, struggling with heavy ropes, were needed to fly them.

A delightful kite ceremony helped celebrate the seventh birthday of a family's first-born son. His father made a kite of straw and provided for it as much string as he could afford or collect. Then, out in the country, he sent up the kite amid prayer and thanks-

In ancient China, an eldest son's seventh birthday was celebrated by sending off his bad luck on a far-flown kite.

giving and carefully payed out the string until the kite was far away, very high—and at the end of its line. This was the moment! With a gesture, the kite was freed so that it flew away, taking with it any bad luck that might have beset the seven-year-old boy. This was the ceremony of Driving Away the Devil.

From Korea, China's neighbor, comes a story that sounds so much like that about the much earlier Huan Theng that it may well be a derivative legend. The troops of a Korean war lord, according to the tale, had lost their morale. To make matters worse, the war lord knew that a formidable enemy was about to engage him. So, like Huan Theng, he arranged for kites to be flown on a very dark night. But he flew the kites over his own troops. From each kite hung a lighted lantern. His henchmen proclaimed, loud and clear, that the lights in the sky bespoke the favor and confidence of the gods. The cheered troops routed the invaders the next day.

7

Kites are common all year 'round in Japan, but May 5—the fifth day of the fifth month—is the traditional day for kites, especially the colorful fish kites which, honoring a family's boys, fly like gaudy wind socks outside Japanese homes.

## IN JAPAN

Kites figure in the most ancient legends and folk tales in Japan. Originally, they were objects of mystery and reverence, but kiteflying soon became popular with both youngsters and adults. The threat of invasion by man-carrying kites must have been feared, however, for there was once a Japanese rule forbidding the construction of kites large enough to carry men.

Evidence of Japan's kite sophistication is revealed in the centuries-old story of Ishikawa Goyamen, a notorious brigand. He coveted the two solid-gold fish that adorned the ridge pole of a temple in Nagoya, but they were on sacred property, well protected, and high above the ground. Aware that there was a fortune perched on the top of the temple, Ishikawa and his gang studied how to get it.

One stormy night, the legend relates, Ishikawa, with

the connivance of his boys, stood in a kind of stirrup attached to a huge kite and went up for the gold fish. The details are sketchy, but despite wild wind and rain, the great kite was somehow maneuvered so that the robber chief could land on the temple roof. At this point the story breaks down. We don't know whether he managed to snitch a gold fin or two or was routed by the temple guard. At any rate, the golden fish remained atop the temple, and Ishikawa faded, tangled in the broken net of legend.

In modern Japan, kiting is practically a national sport. During Boys' Festival, traditionally on May 5, kites by the thousands take the air. Fish kites, similar to the wind socks you see at smaller airports, fly from poles outside the homes of honored sons. Whole families fly elaborate and beautiful kites to show their joy in their man-children.

The Japanese legend of Ishikawa Goyamen relates his attempt, kite-borne, to high-jack golden fish atop a temple.

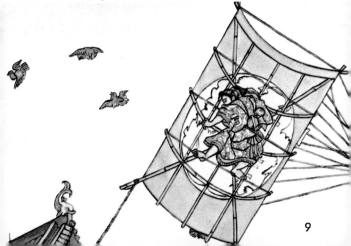

9

# IN THE MEDITERRANEAN

From the Orient, the kite seems to have spread across the world in a devious pattern. Kiting was well known in Egypt, Crete, and Greece. During the Golden Age of Greece, about 400 B.C., a remarkable kite was devised by a serious, scientific-minded man, Archytas, who was a citizen of Athens, a friend of Plato, and several times the military governor of Tarentum, Italy. Not content with ordinary stick-and-cloth or even papyrus kites, Archytas studied the shape and structure of birds' wings. Then he designed and built a bird-shaped kite and flew it on a long cord.

Some say the wonderful old Cretan legend about Daedalus and his son Icarus, the boy who flew on waxen wings too close to the sun, must have had its source in tales of man-carrying kites. It could be.

This map shows the presumed origin and spread of the kite from Asia, first eastward, then, later, into the Mediterranean area.

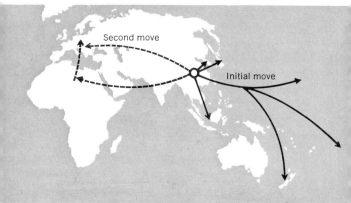

Another legend, Egyptian in source, has to do with two small boys who were trained to fly astride tethered eagles. Considering the technical accuracy and the poetic license of most legends, it seems reasonable to suggest that these brave small boys actually flew on kites. Their purpose was part of a monumental bluff put up by the Grand Vizier of Assyria, called Ahikar. He had been ordered by his Pharaoh to build a palace in the air, somewhere betwixt heaven and earth.

Ahikar took the eagles and their small riders to the Pharaoh and sent them aloft. He had coached the boys to call down to their ruler, "Hail Mighty One! Here we are in the sky, ready to begin your palace. Bring us stone and mortar!" The Pharaoh decided that his true duty to his people was firmly on the ground and promptly canceled his order to Ahikar.

It must be emphasized that the foregoing stories are not only legends, but legends combined with assumptions. From an historian's point of view, therefore, they are very thin.

In fact, there is little evidence that kites were flown in the Oriental fashion in Greece, Egypt, and Italy in ancient times—ceremonially or just for the fun of it. Somewhat later there were flags or guidons that resembled the Japanese fish kites or wind socks, but there is little indication of soaring, self-sustaining kites. Someday, perhaps, scholars will reveal stories of heroic kiteflying from, for example, the Acropolis of Athens. Certainly it would be a reasonable revelation, for the Acropolis is a magnificent kite pad.

Pending possible archeological discoveries it can only be suggested that perhaps Mediterranean life in antiquity was not conducive to the playfulness which is inherent in the making and enjoyment of kites.

# IN EUROPE

Kites underwent a change when they reached Europe. Here they lost their charming mysticism, fanciful decoration, and ceremonial connotations. They became either playthings for boys or devices for serious experiments by adults.

Among the more incredible of these experiments were those made by George Pocock, a schoolmaster in Bristol, England. About 1825, Pocock got the notion that a big kite, or maybe a team of kites, could be made to pull a carriage and its passengers. With teamed eight-foot kites, he actually did manage to tow a light rig and several passengers. For this wind-powered rig, he coined the name *charvolant,* a combination of the French *cerfvolant* (kite) and *char* (carriage).

Obviously the *charvolant* had to go pretty much as the wind listed. Also, trees bordering the road, church steeples, and other obstructions had to be avoided. But three of Pocock's *charvolants* actually did manage to skitter across more than a hundred miles of English countryside, at times reaching the fantastic speed of 25 miles per hour. Pocock's braking system was simply a levered iron spike that was dug into the road when he wanted to stop the *charvolant*. Roads being what they were in those days, Pocock must have contributed substantially to "**better roads**" promotion.

Pocock was one of the first, by the way, to document the fact that the wind is generally stronger and steadier at higher levels. He flew his kites very high from ropes that were unwound from big barrel-like reels fastened to the carriages beside each coachman.

Pocock's idea was picked up by others. There are stories of sailors using high-flying kites to tow their

In 1825, an English schoolmaster, George Pocock, built a "char-volant"—a kite-drawn carriage which achieved a road speed of 25 miles per hour.

boats speedily home from the fishing grounds. Canoes and skiffs are still pulled along by kites. Skaters, bi-cyclists, and swimmers are taken on rides by kites, as are small boys who have made kites too big for them to control.

Pocock also believed that kites could be used to res-cue shipwrecked seamen. To prove his point, he lofted his own son in a kite-borne chair from a beach to the top of a seaside cliff. The trip was smooth and easy. Then the boy got back in his chair, suspended from an iron ring tied to the flying line, and rode his kite seat up into the air, clear of the cliff. To top his act, the boy then untied the light line that held the iron ring securely in place below the kite on the flying line. Ring, harness, chair, and boy then started a long, swift swoop back down the line. Fortunately, the boy's weight made a deep belly in the flying line so that he was moving more slowly as he hit the end of the line. But what a ride! And what a boy!

In the 18th and 19th centuries the first meteorological experiments with kites were made in England and Scotland. Thomas Melville, of Glasgow, sent a thermometer aloft on a kite line and then contrived to cut it loose, trailing a long, identifying streamer. Douglas Archibald, a 19th century Englishman, took wind velocity readings with an anemometer carried far up by a kite. He pioneered, too, in kite photography, using the slow-burning fuse method of shutter release. At about the same time, across the Channel in France, A. Batut used the same method for kite photographs. In kiting, as you may discover, everybody is an inventor or an innovator, despite the fact that someone else may have done the same thing. More fun that way.

During the Boer War, in the late 1890's, six-unit trains of big hexagonal kites were used to carry spotters high over the fighting front. Those kites were the result of a series of experiments and demonstrations by Captain B. F. S. Baden-Powell, brother of the founder of the Boy Scouts.

In 1901 Marconi sent the first trans-Atlantic wireless message—his famous "S" signal—from Cornwall, in southern England, across the Atlantic to a station in Newfoundland. The receiving aerial was carried high in the air by a Baden-Powell kite. More recently, wireless antenna-lofting kites have been included in life raft equipment by the air forces of several countries, including the United States.

Captain B. F. S. Baden-Powell patented his levitor kite, which he used to lift a man a hundred feet into the air. He put his kites to work lifting "spotters" into the air to observe the enemy during the Boer War.

## IN AMERICA

Benjamin Franklin was the first American to make headlines as a kite-flier. In June, 1752, he flew a kite during a storm to prove his contention that the fire of the crackling sky was the same as the electric current that he, among others, had been able to conduct through wires and iron rods. What Franklin did with his kite was extravagantly dangerous but, out of his daring, came new concepts of electricity and, more particularly, a commercially useful device called the lightning rod.

In the American Civil War, bundles of leaflets, broken loose from high-flying kites, were fluttered down over the Rebel troops. They offered am-

To prove his belief that lightning was electricity, Benjamin Franklin flew a kite in a thunderstorm. Electricity traveled down the wet string and could be felt at the end of a key a few feet up the line, beyond a ribbon of nonconducting silk.

Alexander Graham Bell built mammoth kites that consisted of thousands of tetrahedral cells. His largest, towed by a boat, lifted a man.

nesty to those who would lay down their arms. We do not know how effective this kind of propaganda was, but the idea was copied in later wars.

About 1900, Dr. Alexander Graham Bell formed a group that became famous under the name of Aerial Experiment Association. Among its members were Glenn Curtiss, Thomas Selfridge, and J. A. D. McCurdy—each important then and later in the development of aviation. Bell was convinced that the inherent structural strength of the triangle, amplified into a triangular pyramid (a tetrahedron), would produce a super-strong, lightweight framework for a kite—and for, he hoped, a powered flying machine.

Bell and the Association produced in Nova Scotia a mammoth multitetrahedral kite. It was 40 feet wide. Selfridge, later the first American Army man to die in a plane crash, actually flew in Bell's tremendous kite as it was towed along by a powerful boat. He reached an altitude of 168 feet. Later, Bell's kite, called more or

17

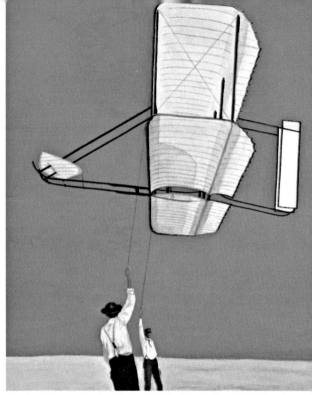

In the strong, steady winds of Kitty Hawk the Wright brothers tested their glider by flying it as a kite.

less appropriately the *Cygnet* (young swan), was tried out unmanned with a motor, but it failed. Glenn Curtiss' *June Bug,* sponsored by the Association, did very much better; it flew with Curtiss as pilot, in 1907.

Bell's tetrahedral kites have a surviving fascination. Almost every year someone shows up with a new variant on the old theme.

18

The Wright brothers, beginning a little earlier, flew kites and experimented with towed gliders. They used a curved or cambered wing, just as old Archytas is alleged to have done, and they built and operated a wind-tunnel to study the relation of wing shapes to lift. Even after their initial successes with powered flight, they returned to Kitty Hawk for further experiments with kites and tethered gliders.

A boy's kite carried the first line across the gorge just below Niagara Falls so that successively heavier lines could, ultimately, pull the first cables of the famous suspension bridge into position. With a huge camera, hoisted by a train of seventeen enormous kites, George R. Lawrence made a spectacular photograph of the ruins of San Francisco after the 1906 disaster. Kite stories, both adventures and misadventures, go far, far back in history.

Even after their first success with powered flight, the Wright brothers used a kite to test their new ideas.

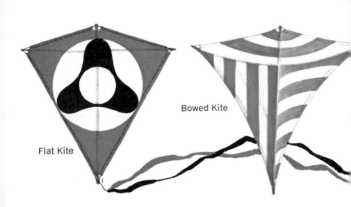

Flat Kite

Bowed Kite

## WHAT IS A KITE?

A kite is not quite an airplane, or even a glider. Nor is it a windmill, a sailboat, or wash flapping on a clothesline. A kite is related to all of these things— but still, it's a little different.

An airplane, with its jet or motorized propeller, forces itself ahead and achieves its support mainly because its speed, relative to the air it encounters, creates a degree of vacuum above the wing. A kite, on the other hand, stands almost still and gains its lift from the wind blowing against, through, and over it. Generally, winds move more slowly than airplanes fly; so the forces acting on kites are neither as strong nor as uniform as those affecting powered planes.

Windmills and kites are cousins. A windmill's angled wings are firmly anchored to the hub; therefore those wings can react to the pressure of the wind by moving in only one way—around and around. A kite is anchored, too, by its line; but unlike the windmill, it can move up, sideways—or even down.

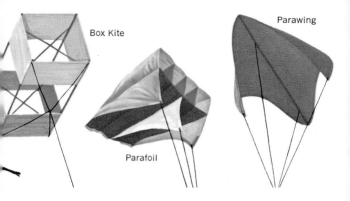

Box Kite

Parawing

Parafoil

Sailboats have tethers called keels. Without its keel a sailboat is helpless, like a kite with a broken line.

Monday's wash on the line is kin to a kite, too. It has a line or a tether, but it doesn't fly. It is not shaped to fly; it is shaped and tethered to flap, which it does.

A kite's essentials are three: first, a wing surface shaped or contrived so that it gains lift from the breeze; second, a line or tether that keeps the kite from being blown helplessly away and, in the process, sets the limits of its flying; and, third, a bridle that holds the face of the kite at an angle to the wind. Lateral and directional stability are secondary.

The bridle is a critical factor. It establishes the kite's angle of incidence or the angle of attack, and for some kites, the attachment of the bridle must be adjusted from time to time as the strength of the wind varies.

Kites can be large or small and of an almost unlimited variety of shapes. Generally, however, they fall into these basic types: flat kites, bowed kites, box kites, **semirigid kites, and nonrigid kites.**

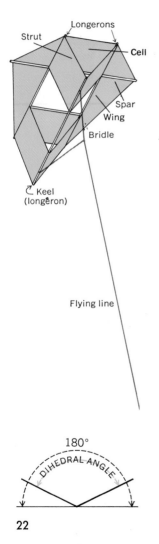

Longerons

Strut

Cell

Spar

Wing

Bridle

Keel
(longeron)

Flying line

180°

DIHEDRAL ANGLE

## A FEW KITE TERMS

Kiting's technical language is not extensive, but definitions of a few terms are helpful.

*Cell.* In the kite shown here, there are two triangular cells. Cells can be square or any symmetrical shape and can be kept open either by struts or by the force of the wind.

*Pocket* refers to the slack in the wing area. Slack on one side must be balanced by pocketing on the other.

*Top,* as used here, is the same as *front. Rear,* the same as *bottom.* To get the idea think of a kite in flight, as the flier sees it.

*Keel* is the longitudinal structural member to which the bridle and the flying line usually connect. In flat kites it may be called the *mast,* or *center pole.*

*Spar,* a transverse stick, usually supports a wing or wings.

*Longeron,* borrowed from the French, is any of the longitudinal members; in some cases the keel is also a longeron.

*Bridle* is the means by which the flying line is connected to the kite; a bridle can have several *legs.*

*Flying line* is just that; it is the kite "string."

*Drag,* the kite's resistance to the wind, is much the same as *pull. Lift,* of course, is the resultant of other forces acting on a kite, mainly the wind and the use made of the wind by the kite's design.

*Dihedral* is the angle formed by two planes that meet, usually, at the keel. It is always less than 180 degrees.

# TO BUY...OR TO BUILD?

Most of the 40 million kites marketed in the U.S. every year are the 25- and 50-cent kites sold in dime stores and supermarkets. But the market for kites costing from two to ten dollars is increasing. One firm sells more than four million such kites. There is a small market for those costing between ten and twenty-five dollars.

Even the cheapest kites, as poorly made as they must be for the price, carry a dangerous virus; it can infect you very easily. All it takes is that trout-like pull of a kite on the line in your hand or the spectacle of a bit of wood and plastic cavorting, siren-like, in the sky. And with cheap kites there is another hazard: they are so easily replaced and so expendable that, before you know what's happened, you are buying kite after kite. In short, you are hooked.

As the price of the kite increases, the construction is better, the shapes and forms more interesting, and the demands on the flier considerably more challenging.

Flat, square-cell box, and "airplane" kites are inexpensive.

A beautiful delta-wing kite in the $5 to $10 class.

Whether you should buy or build your kite is a question that only you can answer. But if you have ever dreamed, drawn, and built your own kite and then achieved with it a successful flight, you have known a great pleasure. The pleasure is multiplied and intensified as your designs, methods, and techniques vary from conventional patterns.

In general, a kiting enthusiast spends much less than a similarly enthusiastic skier, golfer, bowler, motor-rallyist, pilot, or photographer. A kite costing more than twenty-five dollars is indeed rare. The line and a reel for such a kite costs about the same as the kite. So you can begin kiting for as little as half a dollar or spend fifty dollars or more. In time, you will probably acquire more kites, different lines, or heavier reels.

In making your own kites, the cost of materials can be much or little, depending on your choices. You will, of course, spend time, but it will be time well spent. You will certainly learn more about kiting as you build and you will discover also why some kites are better than others.

# KITE-BUILDING MATERIALS

Materials needed for building kites are neither many nor hard to come by. You need wood for spars, struts, keels, and bows, plus paper, cloth, or plastic for the wings. You also need glue and cloth cement, thread, cord, and maybe some poster paints. The only expensive flying line is line that breaks and sends your favorite kite to its destruction.

For the wooden structural members select pieces that are light, strong, flexible, and straight-grained. Spruce, white pine, and even cedar are good. Redwood is straight-grained but brittle, and hard woods are usually too heavy.

Piles of waste may be yours for the asking at your nearest lumberyard. Even ripping a board into small strips is not costly.

Bamboo, because it is usually straight-grained, strong, flexible, and light, is fine for kites. Look for a cane fishing pole or ask a carpet dealer for the bamboo cores on which some rugs are rolled. Cut the bamboo into sections four or five feet long and then, with a stout, sharp knife, start splitting. One pole will give you an ample supply of supple wood for several kites. With a disc sander you can flatten the bamboo "knuckles" easily and cleanly. For extra strength, you can laminate strips of bamboo.

For the Oriental types of kites, the bamboo must be very thin and flexible. One two-dollar bamboo window shade, either matchstick or slat, will give you enough bamboo for dozens of light kites.

Dowel sticks are very useful. They are usually three feet long and supplied in a variety of diameters, from an eighth of an inch up. Select dowels carefully.

Straight wood

Bamboo

Twine

Thread

Glue

Clothespin

Tape

Eyelets

Rings

Grommets

Your pull on the line and the wind's push on its surface give a kite in flight a beating. Construction must be tailored accordingly. Kites that are supposed to be rigidly constructed should have just enough inherent resilience to withstand accidental bad landings. Even semirigid or completely nonrigid kites have to be stronger at such vital points as the flying line connections and shroud attachments. For this reason the light balsa wood so useful to model airplanes is seldom used for kites.

Strong cotton or linen thread will be needed for binding wood-to-wood joints. Glue is used to cement those joints and to fasten down the outline or hem of your kite. A few pinch-type clothespins can be useful for holding things together during construction. Because all glues and cements do not work equally well with wood, cloth, and synthetics, make a few tests. Stripping tape, metal eyelets and grommets, some ordinary twine, sharp-nosed pliers—these are items you are almost sure to accumulate as you go along. Basic to your work, of course, are scissors (pinking shears, preferably) and some really sharp knives.

Paper is most easily available as wing covering. You can get a great variety of paper, but avoid the softer kinds that tear, rip, and crease too readily. You can get rice paper at most hobby shops, but choose the heavier, harder grades. Tracing "cloth" is good, tough —and expensive. Synthetics are suitable for kites, but the cheaper grades tend to tear quickly and, even worse, stretch like putty. Woven synthetics, nylon or dacron, are much better.

If you prefer to use cloth, as most kite makers do, select a material that is easy to handle, light in weight, and so closely woven that it is nearly airtight without doping. Silk, a traditional kite material, is difficult to handle. Cotton "sail cloth" is much better. The finely woven synthetic called Zephyrlite, made especially for the spinnakers of racing yachts, is particularly good. Check among the stocks of combination fabrics (cotton-nylon-dacron, for example) until you find something you like. You'll enjoy the expression on the clerk's face when you say you want all of that perfectly good material for, of all things, a kite!

If you are adept at using the family sewing machine, you can come up with beautifully tailored kites, and nothing beats the strength of well-sewn seams and hems.

In your kite work you will need good straightedges and rulers, a drafting compass, a brace of sharp pencils—and plenty of elbow room. Incidentally, a paper pattern of the proposed kite can save you time and trouble.

Pliers

Knife

Scissors

Cloth

Ruler

Compass

Pencils

27

# CONSTRUCTION METHODS

Only a miracle can give a kite balance in the air if it is unbalanced in construction. Test all the lateral spars carefully. Balance them at their mid-points on a knife edge. You can see quickly where more sanding or whittling is needed. Make it a habit to check and then recheck dimensions as you work.

In kite construction, wood is joined to wood differently than in woodworking. Mortises, deep notches, or even fine holes create weaknesses that cannot be afforded in a kite. The simple cement "welds" of model airplane work are not strong enough for joints that are subjected to the stresses of tethered flight.

A lashed joint is very strong and, if well made, trim. All it takes is a little practice. Sand or shave the areas to be joined—but only enough to assure clean, flat contact. Then, with the two sticks held in position by a vise or a clamp, apply wood glue to both the face and the outside of the joint. Tie the joint tightly with strong thread. Add several windings or lashings, crisscrossing them for uniformity. The glue will seep through the whole binding, of course. With six or eight inches of thread lashed on, set the whole business carefully aside. When it is completely dry, trim off the loose ends and paint the joint with waterproof cement.

Often it will be necessary to notch the ends of sticks so that outlining cord or twine is held in place. But be careful. A notch can start a split. Use a very sharp knife with great discretion. Do not use a saw. Some skilled builders burn-in notches, using red-hot wires or brads to turn the trick. Even with a nicely made notch, it is a good idea to bind the spar. A few turns of thread just inside the notch makes it shipshape.

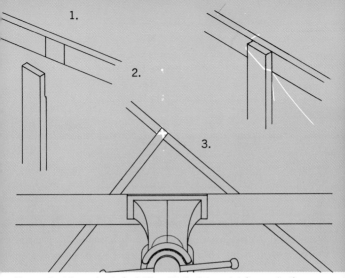

Faces of sticks to be lashed (1) should be smoothed for full contact. Apply glue freely (2) and then tie the joint with strong thread. Use excess thread to bind joint tightly and then paint lightly with more glue. Hold sticks firmly at desired angle in vise (3) until the joint is set. A vise helps.

Check and recheck the dimensions, joint positions, and angles at each step. An error that creeps in will grow with the work.

With reasonably airtight covering material, no final doping to fill or to tauten is needed. Some dopes introduce the hazard of shrinking the material so much it becomes warped. "Dope" is usually a varnish, a lacquer or a shellac that is sprayed or painted on a wing. Use it sparingly. Some large kites seem to be able to tolerate relatively open-pored covering material. Similarly, some kites require a smooth, taut covering, while others fly with slack or pocketing. Only experience and experiment can resolve these mysteries.

## GO FLY A KITE!

Certainly! But where?

A treeless hilltop is ideal. Or a broad beach with a steady offshore breeze. Or a few acres of prairie, your own front yard, a tennis court, a playground, a parking lot, or the roof of a building.

Sometimes such hazards as nearby trees, buildings, or flagpoles cannot be avoided. But some hazards cannot be tolerated. Electric power lines are the worst; streets and highways are almost as bad. Power lines involve not only immediate personal danger but also the more remote possibility of blacking out a whole community. As for highways and similar hazards, it is astonishingly easy to back into a fence, a shrub, or oncoming traffic when you are intent on flying your kite. And a kite, innocently cutting didoes, can also panic drivers with an ill-timed power dive. For these reasons, too, avoid areas under the traffic pattern of an airport. Authorities might clamp down on kiteflying anywhere and everywhere unless kites are flown with care, consideration, and courtesy.

If your kite, however careful and skilled you may be, gets into real trouble, you have two choices. First, try to

fly it out. Let's assume it becomes snagged in a tree. Free the line as much as you can by changing your up-wind angle; then wait for a kindly gust to come along. Unless you have hopelessly entangled your kite by pulling and hauling, the wind and your patience may very well lift it free. The second choice is harsh. Abandon the kite. Don't endanger yourself or all-too-eager small boys by climbing after it or by throwing sticks or ropes at it. Chances are, if it is really snagged, it is also badly damaged. So save as much line as you can, and go back to your drawing board or to the nearest kitery. Your next kite will be a better one anyway.

Bright days with the barometer well up are good flying days. A few clouds do not matter; some fliers deliberately aim for them. But storm clouds, despite Ben Franklin's luck, should be shunned.

WARNING
LOW FLYING PLANES

# ABOUT THE WIND

Some kites fly in almost a dead calm; others survive a gale. Most flying is done, however, with winds in the range from 4 to 18 miles per hour—and the steadier the better. It is useful, though not necessary, to know how fast the wind is moving.

In 1805, Rear Admiral Sir Francis Beaufort devised his classic wind scale for sailors, rating 0 as a dead calm and 12, the top number, as a hurricane. The numbers from 1 to 6, which are germane to kiteflying, can be translated like this:

1. 1 to 3 mph. Smoke drifts lazily.
2. 4 to 7 mph. Tree leaves rustle.
3. 8 to 12 mph. Small flags fly, leaves dance.
4. 13 to 18 mph. Trees toss, dust flies, paper skitters.
5. 19 to 24 mph. Trees sway, kite strings break.
6. 25 to 31 mph. Flying's risky.

You can buy simple, dependable wind meters for a few dollars (the *Dwyer* is one). They eliminate guesswork quite as well as elaborate outfits that cost much money and require fixed installation. The kite-flier's question is really very simple: is there wind enough to fly my kite? Take your kite out and hold it up, by the bridle, facing the wind. If it assumes flying posture, you're in business.

The ground wind and upper wind often differ in velocity, steadiness, and even in direction. But if you can coax your kite up through the tricky ground wind, there comes that magic moment when the true wind takes hold, and your kite soars. If you are in the open the wind's directional variation, usually not more than a few degrees, offers no problem.

# THE FLYING LINE

A few enormous kites require ropes or even hawsers. Some meteorological flying is done with piano wire fed from powered capstans. But wire is expensive, hard to handle, and unforgivably dangerous. A wire line fouled on a power line is lethal.

Here a giant Jalbert parafoil goes up on meteorological duty. For a 20-footer like this, wire cable fed from a winch is necessary.

For flying kites for fun, you may use string, cord, twine, fishing line, mason's cord, twisted or braided nylon or dacron, seine line, waxed bow line, monofilament plastic, tailor's button thread, a spool of thread from the nearest sewing kit—all of these may serve as flying lines. It depends on how strong the line is compared to the expected pull of the kite. Some kite men insist that the line should have a breaking strength four times the anticipated pull. Normally, a 3 to 1 ratio should be adequate.

The joker in this, of course, is that without a fully instrumented wind tunnel you have no really good way of determining how hard a kite is going to pull. Some kites fly *against* the wind and pull hard; others fly more nearly *on* the wind and pull very lightly. And any kite will pull differently as you change the bridle setting. To add to the problem, the power of the wind varies as the square of its velocity.

Here is an arbitrary solution—a completely unscientific rule of thumb: your flying line should have a breaking strength, in pounds, that is at least equal to three times the kite's total frontal area in square feet. Thus, a kite with nine square feet of surface squarely facing the wind needs a minimum of 27-pound line. This falls easily within the range of available lines, most of which are (and certainly should be) clearly marked both as to breaking strength and as to length. Keep in mind that knots in a line tend to cut into and weaken it.

If you are in doubt about a line, hitch one end of it to an anchored spring scale—and pull until the line breaks. Or fix the end of the line under the bathroom scales, stand on them, and pull up. The scale reading at the breaking point, minus your weight, gives you the line's breaking strength.

## KITE-LINE REELS

A kite-line reel can be anything from a stick of wood or a tin can up to a deep-sea fishing reel costing several hundred dollars. Whatever kind of reel you select, remember that rewinding after even the most successful climb can be tedious. So unless the reel has a geared drive, avoid a small core. The larger the core, within reason, the less wear and tear on you.

Except for the most tame flight, you are not likely to bring your kite all the way in, directly to the reel. When the kite gets down into the region of the temperamental ground winds, all you want is a hand (gloved) on the line and freedom to maneuver. So you delegate the winding-in to someone else, or leave it until later. A successful landing of the kite is strictly up to you.

Kite-fliers today tend to use short fishing rods on which are mounted husky, large-capacity reels. A rod-and-reel outfit gives you more than convenience. The rod extends and amplifies your arm movement so that your control over the kite is greater.

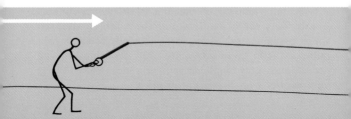

In a good breeze, one-man launch is easy. Back to the wind, cast the kite into the air, giving line as the wind takes hold.

## LAUNCHING

Launching a kite can be frustrating, for the wind has an ornery way of going bad the minute you appear with a kite. You and the wind wage a constant psychological battle.

Some kites require teams and teamwork, but the most enjoyable kites are those you can handle by yourself. They take off from the end of your flying rod or from your hand. With the wind at your back, toss the kite into the air and, as the wind catches it, let out line. As in fishing, don't permit slack, for slack cancels your control. At first, the kite may dart around a bit but by constant small twitches on the line, you can usually manage to keep your kite head up and squarely into the wind. As you pull in on the line you are, in effect, increasing both the topside turbulence and the relative

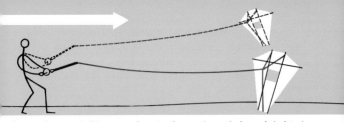

Square-bottomed kites can be stood up, downwind, and hoisted aloft with a quick pull as a gust comes along.

wind speed in the same way that the old-fashioned business of running did. That's why a kite tends to rise as you pull in and fall off as you give it slack.

If the wind is very light, take-offs directly from your hand are seldom possible. You must get the kite well up on the first pull. Walk the kite downwind a hundred feet or so, and either stand it there (box kites have comfortable flat bottoms) or ask a friend to hold it for you while you go back upwind to your reel. Then, with the kite held upright and facing the breeze, wait for a gust. When it comes, your friend yells and launches the kite upward while at the same time you pull in on the line. With luck, the kite will catch a firmer breeze and hold the altitude gained in the first upward rush.

In very light wind (2 to 5 mph.) or with a kite that will not stand alone, ask a friend to hold the kite, about 150 feet downwind. When a gust comes along signal for the release. Then pull in hard.

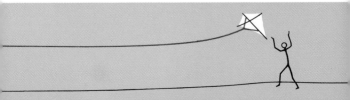

Your hand on the line will tell you when the kite is ready for more altitude; let out line for a second or two, then pull in. In stages, work the kite higher and higher.

Always, of course, there is the chance that the kite will find a steady wind up there. If it does, it will zoom up and out, taking line as fast as your buzzing reel can pay it out. *That* is flying!

But watch out. Such a kite can get into trouble when you halt its "homesick angel" climb, for it then translates its lift into forward motion, swimming smoothly ahead until it reaches the zenith. At this point, depending on the bridling, it is flying almost flat; any pull on the line can put its head under. If the angle of attack becomes a negative angle, something is bound to happen. That "something" is usually a spectacular power dive which, far up, does no harm and is fun to watch. It usually ends in a lateral loop. Then, by line manipulation, you can regain control. At lower altitudes, such a dive can be disastrous.

A kite flying steadily at a high angle is fine, but if it climbs clear to the zenith, watch out!

At the zenith, a kite can nose-under and dive into an outside loop. High up, no harm in it.

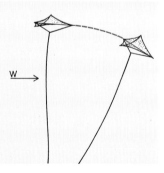
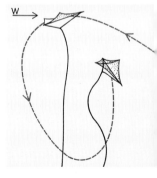

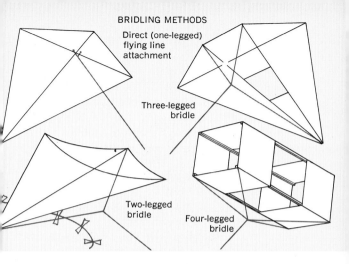

BRIDLING METHODS

Direct (one-legged) flying line attachment

Three-legged bridle

Two-legged bridle

Four-legged bridle

## THE FLYING BRIDLE

The flying bridle and its point of connection with the flying line are the most important and most sensitive of your flight controls. Whether the bridle is two-legged or more-legged, the connecting point determines the kite's flying attitude. Normally, this point is about a third of the way from front to back and about the same distance beneath the keel. In a light wind, a steeper angle of incidence (angle of attack) is needed, so the hitch is made at a lower point. For a strong wind, move the hitch forward. All of this is very simple. A too-low bridle connection, however, may send your kite whooping into a series of uncontrollable lateral loops. A too-high connection can reduce its efficiency so greatly that it flaps like wash on the line.

Experiment to find the optimum setting. Loop into the bridle a series of small solid brass or hard plastic rings (drapery shops are the best sources) about 1 ½ inches apart in the general region of what you know to be the correct place. With a swivel snap fastened at the end of your flying line, you can then change quickly from one ring to another until the best spot is found.

The most effective connection of the bridle line to the flying line, to repeat, is acutely sensitive and important. In a kite of your own making you expect to experiment in locating it. With kites that you buy, you tend to assume that the brass grommet, or eyelet, put in by the manufacturer must be correct, but that is not always true. An eyeleter and a supply of eyelets are essential parts of your kite kit.

All seems serene when your kite is flying high. Some people lose interest at this point because they believe nothing is happening. But a kite is seldom idle and can never be taken for granted, as the whimsical wind can cross you up in seconds. And even though it is thousands of feet up, your kite responds to pulls and twitches on the line. You can make it dance and dive at will. There seems to be a mystical affinity between kite and sun. You will find your kite climbing directly into the sun so regularly that your eyes grow dazzled, your tonsils sunburned.

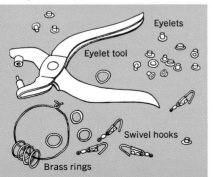

Eyelets

Eyelet tool

Swivel hooks

Brass rings

With eyelets and an eyelet tool (eyeleter), you protect wings from being torn by shrouds.

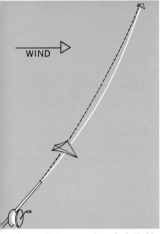
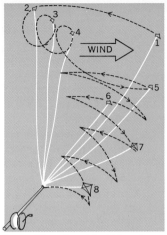

In a light, steady wind (left), kite can be reeled in directly on an almost straight line. In strong wind (right), a flat-flying kite tends to continue seeking the zenith and must be "played in." Reel in as it loops or drifts, hold steady as it climbs, giving line only when necessary. Do not let it loop at low levels.

## LANDING

Landing a kite requires skill and patience. If done successfully, the kite must come in when and where you want it, preferably right to your hand.

The sketches above show how to achieve a good landing in light and strong winds. If your kite insists on looping and diving at low levels, then your best bet is to "walk" it in. Let a friend do the reeling, while you, properly gloved, walk forward with the line under your arm. In this way you shorten the line without actually reeling in. The kite will tend to rise, but if you are careful, you can keep it from going too far until finally it comes to your hand.

41

# HOW HIGH IS UP?

Spectators almost invariably ask (and in kite contests it is important to know), "How high is it?"

The usual response is, very casually, "Oh, about a thousand meters." It's a nice, impressive figure, comprehended by few.

Accurate measurement of a kite's altitude is not easy. Most kites cannot carry recording barographs, and even if you have a good optical range finder, it is seldom possible to make a perfectly vertical reading. A practical solution is possible, however, if you know just two things: how far away the kite is and, second, the angle between the horizon and a line drawn from you to the kite. That line exists, for it is the kite line. If all the line is out, you probably know its length. Or you can mark it with a color code in regular increments.

A height-finder is aimed at a kite. With the length of the line and the angle (indicated by the pendulum) known, the altitude of the kite can be determined from the chart here.

| Angle (degrees) to kite | 100 | 150 | 200 |
|---|---|---|---|
| 05 | 8 | 13 | 17 |
| 10 | 17 | 26 | 34 |
| 15 | 25 | 39 | 50 |
| 20 | 35 | 51 | 70 |
| 25 | 42 | 63 | 84 |
| 30 | 50 | 75 | 100 |
| 35 | 57 | 84 | 114 |
| 40 | 64 | 95 | 128 |
| 45 | 70 | 106 | 140 |
| 50 | 77 | 115 | 145 |
| 55 | 81 | 123 | 162 |
| 60 | 86 | 129 | 172 |
| 65 | 90 | 136 | 180 |
| 70 | 93 | 140 | 187 |
| 75 | 96 | 144 | 192 |
| 80 | 98 | 147 | 196 |
| 85 | 99 | 149 | 198 |
| 90 | 100 | 150 | 200 |

Or, as explained below, you can take a direct reading with an optical range finder.

With the kite's distance known and the angle of its position, you can refer to the table given here to determine the altitude. "Belly" or slack in the kite line affects the accuracy of your calculation somewhat at low altitudes. But the higher the kite and the steeper the angle, the more nearly equal are the distance and the length of the line.

About the optical range finder, a group of Rochester technicians, who sensed a need for range finding in such sports as sailing, hunting, mountain climbing, and even golf, have come up with a remarkably accurate device. They are working on a special adaptation for kiting, but meanwhile, the standard unit, which has a two-mile limit, is very useful. Like other optical instruments, the optical range finder is not utterly foolproof.

**RANGED DISTANCE TO KITE, OR LENGTH OF LINE (YARDS)**

| 50 | 300 | 350 | 400 | 450 | 500 | 750 | 1000 | |
|---|---|---|---|---|---|---|---|---|
| 22 | 26 | 30 | 34 | 39 | 43 | 64 | 86 | |
| 43 | 52 | 60 | 68 | 78 | 87 | 128 | 174 | |
| 64 | 78 | 90 | 100 | 116 | 129 | 193 | 250 | |
| 85 | 103 | 120 | 140 | 153 | 170 | 256 | 340 | |
| 05 | 126 | 147 | 168 | 190 | 211 | 316 | 422 | |
| 25 | 150 | 175 | 200 | 225 | 250 | 375 | 500 | |
| 42 | 169 | 199 | 228 | 256 | 286 | 428 | 570 | Altitude of kite (yards) |
| 59 | 190 | 223 | 256 | 285 | 320 | 480 | 640 | |
| 76 | 212 | 247 | 280 | 318 | 350 | 528 | 707 | |
| 91 | 230 | 268 | 290 | 345 | 383 | 574 | 766 | |
| 04 | 246 | 286 | 324 | 378 | 406 | 612 | 810 | |
| 16 | 259 | 303 | 348 | 389 | 430 | 648 | 860 | |
| 26 | 273 | 317 | 360 | 408 | 451 | 678 | 906 | |
| 34 | 279 | 328 | 374 | 422 | 470 | 704 | 940 | |
| 41 | 288 | 338 | 385 | 434 | 482 | 724 | 965 | |
| 46 | 295 | 344 | 393 | 442 | 492 | 738 | 980 | |
| 47 | 297 | 347 | 396 | 446 | 495 | 744 | 990 | |
| 50 | 300 | 350 | 400 | 450 | 500 | 750 | 1000 | |

# KINDS OF KITES

## THE CLASSIC TWO-STICKER

The two-sticker is the most conventional, the most "kite shaped" kite. Like all flat kites, it requires a tail, and also like most such kites, it flies at a fairly low angle, with maximum drag and minimum lift.

As the drawing shows, you need two sticks: a mast and a somewhat shorter spar. The spar should cross the mast about a quarter of the way down. Center it there and fasten it at a right angle, using either a twisted rubber band or a few windings of thread-and-glue. Outline the kite with string tied to the four stick ends. Do not pull the string so tight that it warps the frame.

Spread out the covering—newspaper, shelving paper, butcher's paper, or any similar paper will do—and position the outlined frame on it. A couple of bits of tape will hold paper and frame together while you draw the outline of the kite on the paper. Make the outline an inch or two oversize so that, when the covering is cut to shape, there will be a margin to fold over and paste down over the outlining string. Notches must be cut in the covering where it fits around stick ends.

The flying line goes through holes in the face of the kite at the central mast-spar joint. To make the kite shipshape as well as to prevent rips, surround the holes with linen reinforcing rings—the sort used for bracing looseleaf notebook paper. The end of the flying line passes through the hole on one side of the joint and comes back out through the diagonally opposite hole. Tie it securely. Two holes on either side of the mast, just inside the bottom hems, give you a tying hold for the tail.

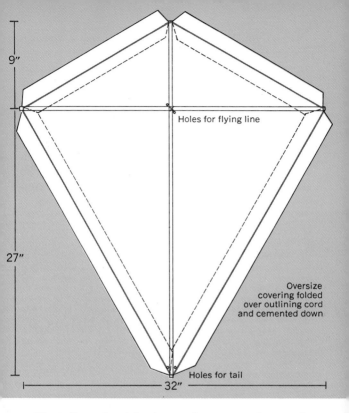

The tail need not be heavy. Its purpose is to resist the kite's naturally skittish tendencies. For a starter, try ten or twelve feet of kite line with crepe paper bows tied into it every foot or so. Flight tests will indicate whether the tail is too short or too long.

Kite tails are not intended to provide balance in terms of weight, which only makes a kite sluggish. Tails add drag, or resistance, allowing the kite to soar freely.

45

Unless you have a wind of 8 or 10 mph, you will probably need the help of a friend to get this kite airborne. The tail should be stretched out on the ground downwind of the kite so that, from the start, it is effective as a balance. If you have to run with this kite, as will almost certainly be necessary in very light winds, go to it.

Vary the dimensions shown as much as you please; nothing about this kite is very critical. Resist temptation to make it really big. The results are unrewarding. Flat kites may be primitive, but they are never dull. And they can be of almost any shape, size, or material.

**THE TWO-STICKER** In making your kite, you should (1) notch the spars to hold the outlining cord and bind the notched ends to prevent their splitting. The covering (2) should be cut away at the corners, allowing at least an inch of fold-over for cementing. The line or bridle (3) is connected at the central mast-spar joint, with gummed reinforcement circlets used to protect the covering around the holes. The flying line (4) can be connected directly or by means of a one-legged bridle. The connection is made easy with a loop and a fishing swivel. A swivel belongs on the end of every flying line.

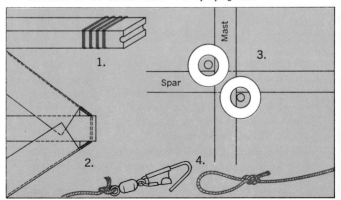

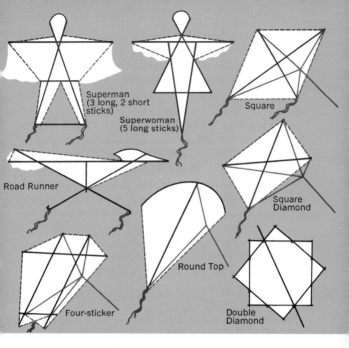

Superman
(3 long, 2 short sticks)

Superwoman
(5 long sticks)

Square

Road Runner

Square
Diamond

Four-sticker

Round Top

Double
Diamond

## MORE FLAT KITES

Flat kites are popular because they are easy to make and lend themselves so readily to wild decoration. Moreover, with their necessary tails, they are charming to watch as they sashay across the sky. They can be almost any reasonably symmetrical shape.

As the drawings indicate, these flat kites can be two-, three-, or even four-stickers. Do not, however, bind more than two or three sticks together in a single joint. The thickness of such a joint destroys the essential flatness of your kite and complicates its flight.

One of the best of these flat kites is a hexagonal three-sticker; its two masts cross and are joined at a point a little above their centers, and the spar goes across slightly higher still. Bind the joints, outline the kite, cover it—and now you are ready for your first variation in flying line attachment.

First create a bridle by means of a length of twine tied through the kite face at each of the two joints of the spar and the uprights. The midpoint of this bridle is your flying line connection. A similar line, linking the lower ends of the uprights, gives you opportunity to attach a sliding tail harness. All it amounts to is a ring that slides freely and to which the tail is tied.

After you have tried a few flat kites, you will begin to ponder what happens when you bow the flatness back, with a taut line from wing tip to wing tip. You are then ready for the next phase of kite making.

Hexagonal three-sticker can be made with straight sticks (A) or with bent center sticks (B). Note low vent in A, and at top, bottom, and above vent in B. Both need a long tail.

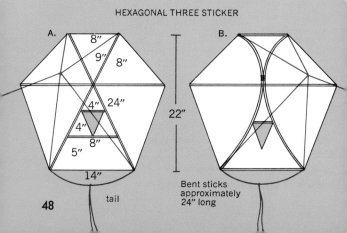

HEXAGONAL THREE STICKER

A. 8" 9" 8" 8" 4" 24" 4" 8" 5" 14" 22" tail

B. Bent sticks approximately 24" long

48

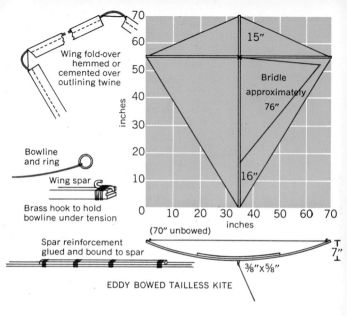

EDDY BOWED TAILLESS KITE

## THE BASIC BOWED KITE

Converting a flat kite into a bowed kite introduces an aerodynamic factor called dihedral or dihedral angle —the angle formed at the meeting of two supporting planes. In a kite, the dihedral is the angle, at the keel, between the outspread wings. It is usually a very flat "V." Birds have a dihedral angle. So do airplanes. And in one form or another, many fine kites have a dihedral, too.

The most famous bowed two-stick kite was designed, built, and flown in the 1890's by William A. Eddy, of Bayonne, N.J. Eddy's kite looks simple—and really is.

Eddy kites look very simple; actually they repay accuracy and fine workmanship with good performance. An 8-footer like this, by J. W. Aymire, develops great pull.

But to perform well, it must be made with great precision. There must be a degree of pocketing in the wings as they are bowed back. Without this pocketing, you may become so frustrated with the kite's performance that you may be tempted to add a tail. But Eddy kites are tailless!

A variation of the Eddy design is the double-bowed three-sticker. It has a stubbier design, but it flies well. The trick in making this kite is to obtain identical and parallel configuration in both top and bottom bows.

Unlike flat kites, the bowed kites can be scaled up to very considerable sizes. Some of the best Eddys being flown today are more than six feet tall.

# BOX KITES

The box kite is to kiting what the biplane was, and is, to powered aviation. It is strong, it has doubled wing surface, and its conformation creates a lot of drag.

From the start, the box kite was a workhorse. Invented by an Australian, Lawrence Hargrave, about 1892, it was put to work almost at once by U.S. government meteorologists. They sent it far up carrying all sorts of recording instruments. Sometimes, in order to loft especially heavy loads, box kites were flown in tandem, in teams, or even, as the French say, *en train*. Men, big cameras, huge flags, fireworks—all sorts of items were sent up just for the novelty of it.

Early Hargrave box kites, as shown below, were so steady that they inspired pioneer plane builders—Farman, particularly—to adapt them for powered flight.

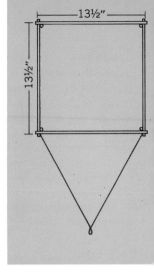

A conventional square-cell box kite tends to be more stable when flown "on edge" than the same kite when flown flat.

But don't get the idea that box kites are dull drudges. They can be giddy as goats. A box kite can be of almost any size, but do not go in for six-foot box kites until you have learned to handle three- and four-footers.

Mr. Hargrave's original box kite incorporated two elongated rectangular boxes or cells. The forward (upper) cell was of a little less total area than the rear. It flew, of course, with the long sides of its boxes parallel with the horizon. The tendency today is away from elongated boxes and toward formalized designs in which both cells of the kite are square and are of equal size.

The engineering of a box kite depends on the type of kite you want—whether rigid or collapsible. The rigid box is more conventional in its construction and covering. It is also a bit stronger and considerably

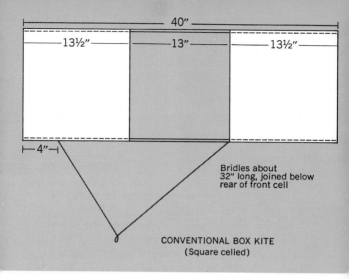

Bridles about
32" long, joined below
rear of front cell

CONVENTIONAL BOX KITE
(Square celled)

more ungainly to cart around. The collapsible type involves a few tricks, especially in the covering. It is, of course, easy to tansport.

The basic, square-section box kite has four essential structural members—the longerons, which are all the same length, thickness, and weight. In the rigid type of construction, the square-sectioned "boxes" are established by bound-and-glued squares of split-bamboo sticks (or whatever kind of sticks you prefer to use). Some builders use four such sections, thus firmly establishing the outlines of the two boxes. Others use three squares—one at the center, the other two about midway of the cells. The determining factors are the strength, weight, and size of the structural materials. You can save weight in this manner on kites less than three feet long, but in larger kites strength is vital.

Ray Biehler's winged box kite, constructed of aluminum tubes and with hinges to permit folding, is flown with a "deep sky" reel.

Covering a rigid, fully sectioned box kite is a cinch; you can do it with glue or cement, making the usual allowances for fold-over margins and "V"ed cut-outs at the corners. If you elect to use three rather than four structural squares, the upper and lower edges of the covering material should be hemmed or cemented down over string that connects all four longerons.

If you prefer a nonrigid box kite, construction begins with the covering, preferably cloth of some sort. Make two panels which, after hemming, are long enough to include all four sides of the cells or boxes, plus an inch or so to provide for sewing the ends together; the width of these panels should be, after hemming, the full longitudinal depth of each cell. For a box kite three feet long with two cells a foot square and a foot deep, the two panels should each measure one foot by four feet, plus that inch or so for joining.

At this point you must decide how the cells are to be kept open and square. The easiest solution is to make a series of flexibly joined X's of wood, the two crossing members of each X being as long as the diago-

nal of the squared cells. For a one-foot-square cell, the diagonals would be just a whisker under 17 inches. The joint (the crossing of each X) can be bound with a rubber band, and the ends of each stick should be notched to embrace the longerons. Make these sticks just a bit longish, so that they fit very tightly. If you use bamboo sticks, they will flex enough to serve your purposes.

Let's assume you have made three or four of these internal X's and fitted them snugly into position. Stand the box up on the ends of its longerons, and check it carefully for alignment and trueness. When you are satisfied that the box is all squared up, you can fasten the longerons to the covering with short strips of masking tape.

All that remains now is to attach the bridle. First, you must decide whether your kite is to fly flat (that is, with two sides of each cell parallel with the horizon) or on edge (with one of the longerons serving as keel). You get more lift from the former and greater stability from the latter.

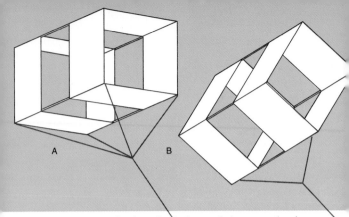

Shown here are the four classic forms of the conventional square box kite. A is the kite flown "flat," with a four-legged bridle. B shows the kite flown on edge, with a simple, two-legged bridle. In

The bridling of a flat-flown box kite is usually four-legged. Actually, it consists of two lengths of flying line attached to the diagonally opposite ends of the two frontal longerons. The lines should be precisely the same length and loose enough so that they can be joined at a point about a foot below the rear edge of the front cell.

For edge-flown box kites a two-legged bridle is indicated. It is attached to the ends of the keel longeron or, possibly, at points along the keel about midway of each cell. Small box kites may be flown from a single connector fastened to the keel at the rear of the front cell, but a two-legged bridle gives firmer control and permits flying under more variable conditions.

You can add considerable lift to a box kite with outboard wings that are attached to a spar running across

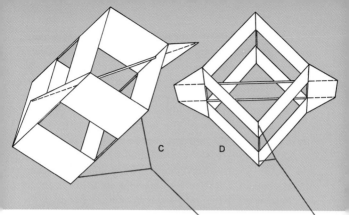

C, a horizontal wing has been added to the edge-flown kite, with a spar running through the upper cell to support the wing. D is the same as C but has two supporting spars for the larger "stub wings."

the upper box or, in the case of edge-flown kites, diagonally through or just below the upper cell. This spar is seldom longer than twice the diagonal of the cells. It must be fairly strong. If it is fastened to the underside of the longerons, it need only be held with a rubber band tie or even a twist of tape. Notch the ends of the spar to hold the outlining cord and then proceed as in ordinary kite construction.

The cellular design of box kites keeps them turned into the wind automatically. You will find that they pull hard at low levels and tend to float when they get well up. Two or more box kites can be lashed together to create quite monstrous affairs. But such stunts can wait until you've earned your box kite wings; as it happens, there are enough standard variations on the box kite theme to keep you busy for a long time.

Another variation, expressly for edge-flown boxes, involves the elongation of four of the cell-forming struts. On these extended struts, reaching out and up from the keel, additional wing area is very easily hung. The result is a box kite with an exaggerated dihedral angle. And it's not a bad flier, either.

The stub-winged box kite is a variation you should know about, partly because it is so reliable and partly because it figured in an attempt to fly the Atlantic by kite. A few years ago, "Scotty" Scott and Benn Blinn figured that an inherently stable kite could be induced to climb aboard the prevailing westerlies out of New England and fly away to Ireland or thereabouts. Because a conventional kite line was a bit impractical, Scotty and Benn came up with a stunning idea: a kite line that provided the correct drag but went right along with the east-bound kite. To achieve this, they tied partially filled gallon jugs to the end of the line. After a few trials, the correct weight was determined and off went eighteen stub-winged box kites toward Europe. To date, according to Scotty, one of those kites has arrived at its destination.

The stub-winged box kite is an edge-flown square-section box kite, with spars for the outboard wings di-angling across the square sections, both upper and lower. It packs a great deal of wing area into a relatively compact, stable shape. It is indeed a reliable, workhorse kind of kite; Scotty and Benn had good reason for selecting it for the trans-Atlantic effort.

Box kites have been made also with triangular cells, round cells, and ovate cells. But forget the last two. They fly poorly.

Mr. Hargrave's original box kites were rectangular in section and the two cells differed in area, with the

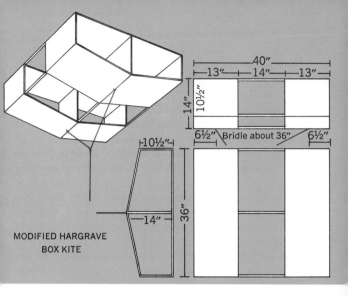

MODIFIED HARGRAVE
BOX KITE

front the smaller. Followers of this concept will assure you that the larger rear cell acts as a weathervane and keeps the kite strictly headed windward; others insist that all that weathervaning is not needed and that the larger cell should be in front where it carries most of the load, with only a balancing assist from the junior partner out back.

Ray Biehler, a Rochester physics teacher, built a box kite for flying from the deck of a yacht. It is a six-foot masterpiece, executed in aluminum tubing (pp. 54-55). Thanks to beautifully machined little hinges, the whole kite folds up, umbrella fashion. Rolled up, it looks like a bazooka. It is a square box design, with the spar for the outboard wings going right across the top of the upper cell. It would be a masterpiece even if it couldn't fly, but it flies beautifully.

59

# THE TRIANGULAR BOX KITE

The idea of the triangular box kite is exactly like that of the square box kite, except that the two cells are equilateral triangles rather than squares. As compared to a flat-flown square box kite, the triangular box kite has only half as much wing area flat to the wind. But because two-thirds of its total area is in the "V's" of the triangular cells, it gains in stability, and the slanting sides contribute lift. All in all, the triangular box kite is pretty efficient.

By adding a spar across the upper cell to support a pair of outboard wings, the lift is increased, and the stability of the built-in dihedral is retained. This results in a remarkable kite.

An American, Silas J. Conyne, worked out the design for this kite and patented it, in 1902. The French army recognized the kite's values and put it into military service. Consequently, this kite is better known today as the French Military Box Kite than as the Conyne Kite.

The triangular-box-kite-with-wings is strong, stable, and a high-angle flier. It can be built rigidly, with fixed wings and bound joints, or non-rigidly so that it can be dismantled and rolled to fit into a tube. The rigid style is strong but bulky. The folding kite is more convenient to cart around but trickier to make—mainly because its covering, usually cloth, must be so precisely tailored. Both forms follow the dimensions shown.

The three-footer is a good size for a starter. Even rigidly built it can be stowed in the back seat or trunk of a car. Dowel sticks usually come in three-foot lengths, so your longerons are ready-made. Use 3/16-inch dowels, if available. If not, 1/4-inch dowels will do.

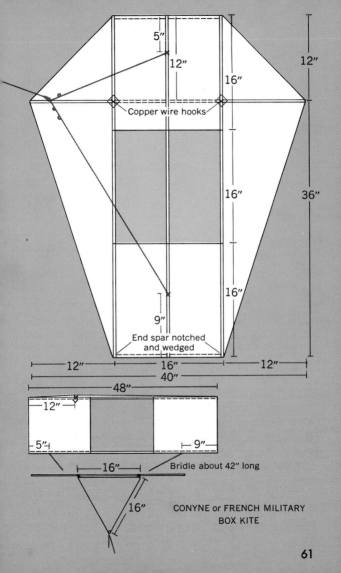

5"

12"

12"

16"

Copper wire hooks

16"

36"

16"

16"

9"

End spar notched
and wedged

|←— 12" —→|←— 16" —→|←— 12" —→|
|←————————— 40" —————————→|

|←————————— 48" —————————→|
|←12"→|

5"                          9"|

|←— 16" —→|
Bridle about 42" long

16"

CONYNE or FRENCH MILITARY
BOX KITE

A fleet of French Military (Conyne) Box Kites, all different in number of spars, in rigidity and bracing, and in positioning of spars. Only

For the spar that traverses the upper cell and supports the outlying wings, use at least a ¼-inch dowel. Even so, it may have to be reinforced; it will get a lot of stress. A thin strip of bamboo, bound and glued to the back of the spar, will probably give it sufficient reinforcement for ordinary flying.

Covering any three-dimensional kite is difficult, even with paper and paste. For safety, make your first Conyne kite rigidly. Cover it with rice paper after the frame is complete. Be sure to provide ample margins for fold-overs and "V" notches at the corners so that

a single bridle arrangement is shown, but this can be varied as flight tests may suggest.

the paper can be securely cemented down on the back and will fit neatly. These kites, by the way, should be taut and trim, with minimum sagging or pocketing.

If you elect to build a folding Conyne kite, your first job is to make the two triangular cells. Assuming that you will be using cloth, make two panels, each of which is long enough to fit all the way around the cells. If your cells are one foot on each side, you'll need panels three feet long. Provide an inch or so for joining. Hem the edges of the panels to size. Both panels should be identical in size and shape.

Notched equilateral "Y's," force-fitted against longerons, can be used to keep triangular cells open and taut.

To make the kite completely shipshape, make three sleeves or pockets, accurately spaced, to receive the three longerons. Some kitemen prefer to use internal bracing to keep the cells open and properly shaped up; others depend on the opposing forces of lift and the pull of the kite line to keep the cells open. If you favor internal bracing, build a brace of demountable "Y"s to force-fit against the longerons. The ends of the "Y" braces should, of course, be notched so they can't slip off.

Whichever way you build your Conyne, the upper panels of the two cells—these are the panels that fly flat—have to be kept well opened. The wing spar, connected to the two upper longerons with twists of copper wire, takes care of the upper cell. The lower cell needs only a one-foot internal spar, which should be suitably notched.

In flight, the nonrigid kite is kept open by the two opposing forces of the flying line, which pulls earthward, and the lift of the wings. With the rigid type, there is no such problem, of course.

The bridle is fastened securely to the keel longeron, either at its ends or midway of the two cells. It must

This is a birdlike variant of the Conyne triangular box kite. The long, birdlike wing is inherently flexible.

be at least as strong as the flying line and long enough to provide about a foot of slack. As usual, the flying line attachment is about a third of the way from the front (or top). You will discover the optimum point by making a few test flights.

A three-foot Conyne, with a total of five square feet of wing area flat to the wind plus four more at a 60-degree angle, should be flown with a line that has a breaking strength of at least 21 pounds. A little more, say 25, would be safe. The breeze required for the kite's flight will depend somewhat on the weight of your finished kite. Five mph should be about the minimum. If the wind is 10 mph or more, adjust the bridle connection forward a bit so the kite flies more nearly level. Otherwise the kite may be torn apart by the brute force of its drag.

Like most kites, the triangular box kite lends itself to endless variation. It can be made as large as you like, but anything beyond six feet becomes definitely a two-man kite. The real secret of the Conyne design is that it combines considerable strength with a built-in and constant dihedral angle, one of the best stabilizing factors.

# TETRAHEDRALS AND TRIANGLES

The box or cellular concept in kite design has been played with by countless enthusiasts, but most of them have agreed that the principle of diminishing returns applied as elaboration increased. With complexity piled on complexity, the kite became relatively heavier, and the frontal area built up monumental drag. Flying ability dropped.

Alexander Graham Bell's tetrahedral kites provide the classic example. A tetrahedron is a triangular pyramid; it has three sides and a base. Dr. Bell's basic unit was a pyramid composed of four equilateral triangles. Two of the sides, or planes, were open, and two were covered. The two adjoining covered planes were the wings. But those two neat little triangular wings had to carry the rest of the unit, which required six sticks or spars to hold it together. This was quite a burden, so a single-unit tetrahedron kite was not very efficient. Dr. Bell discovered that by combining a number of units, single spars could be made to serve several neighboring units. Both structural and flying efficiency were increased.

Encouraged, the inventor then proceeded to create tremendous constructions, made up of hundreds of units or cells. His 40-foot *Cygnet* (pp. 17, 18), though it was certainly no swan, did fly and did carry a man nearly two hundred feet into the air. But it took a strong wind and a powerful boat to tow it, because the complex construction created tremendous frontal resistance and drag. Today we have motors powerful enough to fly the *Cygnet,* but we have outgrown our reliance on interlocked tetrahedrons for strength. The current trend is toward simplicity and easy portability.

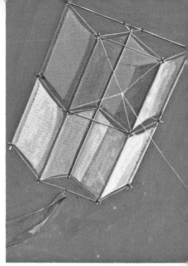

This neat little W-format kite is available in do-it-yourself kit form. Tail is more decorative than functional.

Still, tetrahedral kites have a lot of fascination. If you make one, limit yourself to four- or seven-unit combinations at the start. Otherwise, you can easily find yourself involved with a monster that you may not be able to get out of the shop, much less into the air.

You may want to try a variation on Dr. Bell's tetrahedral idea which, remember, assumed four joined equilateral triangles. Both area and efficiency will be gained by using right-angle triangles. Depending on their proportions, the dihedral angles will be flatter, and you will get improved lift.

All sorts of shapes can be combined—triangles, squares, rectangles, circles, cylinders, and so on. But complexity begets complexity—and as the weight-lift ratio rises, your chances of seeing your laboriously concocted kite sail serenely in the blue become drearier and drearier.

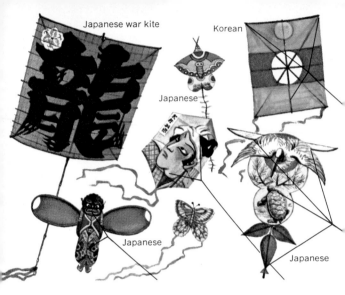

Japanese war kite

Korean

Japanese

Japanese

Japanese

## ORIENTAL KITES

Kites produced in Malaysia, in the various countries of India, in China, and in Japan all have their distinctive differences. On the whole, they tend to be differences of flying attitudes rather than basic format. An Indian sportsman buys his kites from professional kite makers and flies them competitively to knife his rivals from the air. Chinese and Japanese kites are flown, generally, either for the fun of it or in accord with some established ceremonial.

The common denominators of Oriental kites are bamboo and paper, for both are readily available and make excellent kites. Because bamboo is beautifully bendable and paper (usually rice paper) so easily dec-

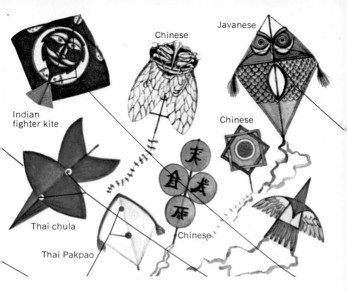

Indian
fighter kite

Chinese

Javanese

Chinese

Thai chula

Thai Pakpao

Chinese

orated, it is entirely in character for Oriental kites to be made in all sorts of complex shapes and painted in wild designs and color combinations. A perfectly plain, undecorated Oriental kite is unthinkable.

Oriental kites are mostly flat kites. It follows that they need tails. Indeed, the long, luxurious, sweeping tails are frequently as decorative as the kites themselves.

### The Fighter Kite

Do not be fooled by the fighter kite of Malaya or India. It is not as simple as it appears. Actually, it is a sophisticated combination of lines, stresses, and subtle variations. Really good fighter kites are made by professionals who build into them clever refinements that are not obvious. Some of these subtle differences have come down through time as family secrets. The true fighter kite is superficially a flat kite, but it flies without a tail, which would be an impediment. The fighter kite depends on its own exquisite balance and the skill of its flier to keep it in the air and under control.

Structurally, the fighter kite is a two-sticker, with a sturdy keel and a delicately flexed spar. Great care must be used in shaping and balancing the spar, which is thinner at the ends than at the center where it joins the keel. In some forms, the top of the spar is slightly rounded. As shown in the illustration, there is an inverted "V" outlined in light bamboo at the bottom of the keel, the suggestion of a built-in tail.

The paper is so much a part of this kite's structure that the process of applying the covering cannot be casual. After the keel and the spar are joined at a spot about a seventh of the way from the top of the keel and the vestigial tail is cemented in position, set them aside and concentrate on making the flat, diamond-shaped wing. This must be done as accurately as possible. Cut the paper about a quarter or three-eighths of an inch oversize all around, and make the pasting fold smooth and shipshape. Outline the whole kite with a very light thread, neatly encased by the folded-over edges. Fasten the paper, accurately centered, to the full length of the keel, and cement down the fold-overs of the "tail" and the two lower edges.

When the adhesive is set, bend the curved wing spar gently down so that it fits within and is held by the fold-overs of the upper two edges. This is a tricky process, for the arc of the wing spar and its tension must be the same on both sides. Work on a flat, firm surface so that the wing will not have bulges, wrinkles, or other signs of unequal stress. While the wing spar is being cemented into the wing edges, you may have to hold onto the whole kite while the adhesive takes its grip. Do not use tape to hold rice paper in position. It tears.

Now you have what appears to be a good, flat, diamond-shaped wing. Suitably bridled, you reason, such a kite would fly, but it would certainly need a tail. Purists insist otherwise, however, so try flying it. If the kite refuses to behave, even with your most delicate and cunning handling, your first recourse is to add a bow string.

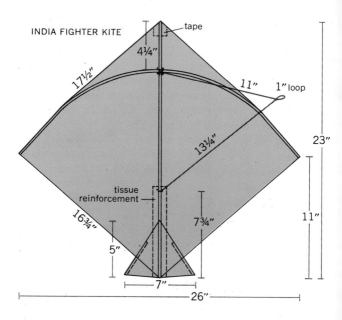

The bow string runs across the kite's back from wing tip to wing tip, with just enough tension on it to bow the kite an inch or so. If flight remains only a vain fluttering even when the kite is bowed, swallow your pride and attach a tail. Now it will probably fly, but you no longer have a simon-pure fighter kite.

Fighter kites are generally 14 to 18 inches on a side. If made larger they tend to lose some of their swift, darting quality. It's an interesting fact that, for all sorts of fine technical reasons, some kite designs —such as the India fighter kite—resist enlargement.

The classic India fighter kite is flown with a line covered with bits of broken glass in paste. Such a line slashed across a rival's line can cut it down. But that's the name of the game.

## Dragon Kites

At the other end of the kite spectrum from fighter kites are the ponderous dragon kites. But dragon kites are certainly spectacular and well worth trying, especially as a club project, in camps, or similar groups. In some languages, *kite* literally means dragon, so the Chinese call this creation the centipede kite.

The dragon or centipede kite's basic characteristic is that it is comprised of a face or a head and as many body segments as you can manage to build and get airborne. In some forms, the body segments are all the same size. Classically, the segments dwindle in size from front to back. Almost always, the head is about half again as large as the largest body segment.

The head is a flat kite—round, hexagonal, ovate, or any shape that appeals to you. The covering is almost always paper, primarily because paper takes paint so well. The face *must* be painted, and the more fiercely the better to make this kite a real frightener.

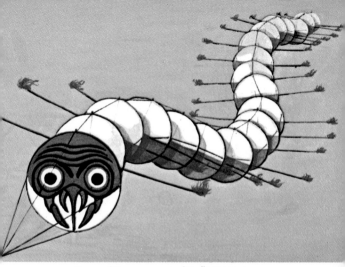

Dragon kites are supposed to float away
evils which might attack the owner.

**Because the face unit has to tow all the rest of the**
beast, make the face kite a little larger and sturdier
than the others. If the face is two feet in diameter,
then the first body segment back of it should be about
18 or 20 inches in diameter. Each successive segment
should decrease in size an inch or two.

Each segment is made of a circle of bamboo, with a
brace or spar running across its upper third. This
spar extends beyond the covered circle and is decorated, at both ends, with a spray of colored tissue
strips. Everything about this kite is calculated to contribute to the general sense of wriggle, flutter, and
writhe. Some dragon kites even include wildly rolling
eyes—clever mechanisms in themselves—to add a
final touch of terror.

The great, long animal is held together by four lines extending back from the face kite. One joins the tops of the train of segments, another joins the bottoms, and the two others connect with the spars of the several segments at the points where they emerge from the circles. The spacing between the units of the dragon decreases with their size, beginning with an interval of about 20 inches.

The bridle may be either a three-legger, or, preferably, a four-legger. In both, two of the legs are extensions of lines connecting the ends of the spars.

Of these three animal kites, only the bird really flies. The fish and the cobra are essentially ceremonial wind socks.

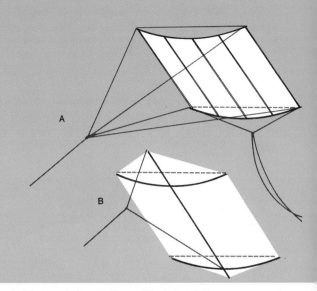

Two double-bowed kites, similar but with significant differences. Kite A, sometimes called a Japanese War Kite, is a rectangle in the proportions of 3 wide by 4 high, with the upper and lower spars bowed back by taut lines running from spar-end to spar-end. Even so bowed, a tail is usually necessary, plus a four-legged bridle. It pulls hard, is swift and not always predictable. Needs a 5-mile wind.

Kite B is of the same general proportions, somewhat elongated by the peaking of the wing, fore and aft, on the extended keel. Bow lines hold both spars. It is really a simple three-stick bowed kite, structurally less complicated than the War Kite. (Still, getting and keeping those spars lined up is quite a trick.) It needs no tail and flies on a two-legged bridle. A 3-mile wind should suffice.

Flying the dragon, or centipede, is definitely a team operation, and the bigger the kite the greater the need for teamwork. You may need two men on the line and three others to help hold the ungainly beast in position for take-off. A breeze of between 7 and 10 mph is needed.

This is a kite for very special occasions. Because it is a ceremonial kite it should be as wildly decorated as possible. Horns, ears, fangs, whiskers, and bulging eyes can be added to the face, and the trailing body

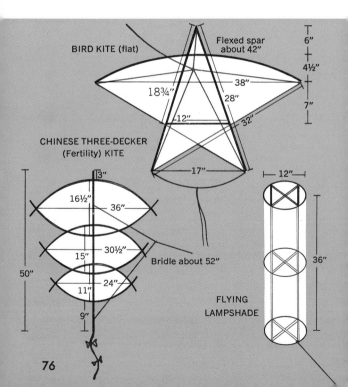

BIRD KITE (flat)

Flexed spar about 42"

6"

4½"

38"

18¾"

28"

7"

12"

32"

CHINESE THREE-DECKER
(Fertility) KITE

17"

3"

12"

16½"

36"

15"

30½"

Bridle about 52"

11"

24"

50"

36"

9"

FLYING
LAMPSHADE

76

should have lots of raw color. You may not achieve a high-altitude flier with one of these kites, but you should certainly create a spectacle.

By combining circles, squares, lean or fat triangles, and ellipses, kite shapes are unlimited in the Oriental fashion. They need only be symmetrical and capable of being executed in light bamboo and tissue or rice paper. You may also find suitable covering material in the gift wrapping left over from birthdays and holidays. Choose the bolder designs and colors.

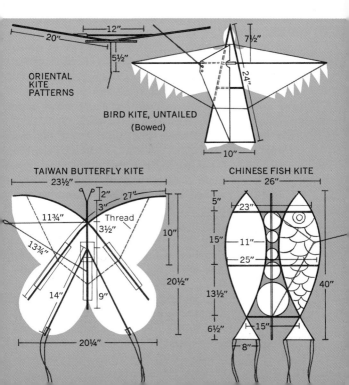

ORIENTAL KITE PATTERNS

BIRD KITE, UNTAILED
(Bowed)

TAIWAN BUTTERFLY KITE

CHINESE FISH KITE

# SLEDS IN THE SKY

Now, after thousands of years of subtle variations on classic themes, there has been an outburst of new ideas and new forms in kites.

One of the most successful of these new kites is the Scott sled. It was evolved by Frank Scott, son of "Sir Walter" Scott, one of kiting's several unique characters. Frank's kite is called a sled for the simple reason that, in the air, it resembles a snow sled. It has no lateral stiffening, so it can be rolled up and carried easily in a tube. Unroll it, shake it out, attach the flying line—and you are ready for flying.

An interesting feature of this kite is that it resists variation. True, the triangular vent can be inverted or made into a circle but, even so, the proportions hold remarkably steady. Sleds as small as 18 inches long have been built and flown successfully, but the basic three-footer is the most reliable performer.

As the drawing indicates, the "structure" of the sled consists of three slender (1/8") three-foot dowels. The wing can be all one piece, or if you prefer, the "runners" can be made of a contrasting color. All of the edges should be hemmed or turned over and cemented, but no outlining cord is necessary. Fasten the dowels to the wing (rather than vice versa) with tabs of pressure-sensitive tape. After you have set grommets or eyelets into the apexes of the runners, you are ready to rig the long, two-leg bridle, clip on the flying line— and take off.

The length of the bridle lines is critical. If they are too short, they tend to pull the laterals (the runners) together; if too long, they permit the laterals to flare out and lose their directionally stabilizing value. Sleds

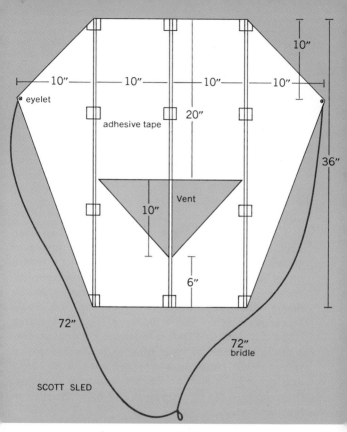

10"

10" 10" 10" 10"

eyelet

adhesive tape

20"

Vent

10"

36"

6"

72"

72"
bridle

SCOTT SLED

can be flown with very light monofilament line, but it is safer to use a light braided line. The arbitrary rule for line strength (p. 34) suggests a line in the 15- to 18-pound bracket.

Sleds can be capricious. The big trick is getting them up out of the ground winds, and this feat may at times leave you purple with frustration.

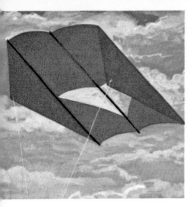

Scott sleds are at their best in light, steady winds and in thermals. They fly at an angle of 60 degrees or higher and have a relatively light pull. Flying a Scott sled is not child's play, but it is a distinct pleasure.

Sleds have the maddening tendency to fold up when a gust or a cross wind hits them, and once folded or closed, they fly like bricks. If you are tempted to add a bit of lateral stiffening (and practically everyone is), restrict it to a strip of light cardboard, rattan, or the thinnest sheet balsa about 16 inches long. This should be centered an inch below the top of the central panel.

As soon as a sled finds a reasonably steady breeze, it really needs no stiffener other than the firmness of your control. Never give it unrestricted slack. Feed line out only as fast as the kite will take it without flapping. After the sled is well up (but not until), you can take chances.

In flying a Scott sled, keep it well up—at an angle of at least 35 degrees. Below that, it pulls very hard, but its balance is precarious. It has even been known to lateral-loop.

Scott sleds are at their best in light, steady winds and in thermals. They fly at a very high angle, 60 degrees or higher, and have a relatively light pull. Flying a sled is not child's play, but it is a pleasure.

A paperfold kite soars serenely on sewing thread line.

## PAPERFOLD KITES

You should know about folded paper kites. There is nothing like them for lifting the spirits. You can design, produce, and have a paper kite airborne in a couple of minutes. All you need is a sheet or two of paper (typewriter bond is fine), a small stapler, scissors, and a spool of ordinary sewing thread.

There are dozens of paperfold designs, some of which are patented. Most fly very well. The best design I know has the triangular shape of the paper darts or gliders every schoolboy makes. It has no sticks, fins, rudders, tails, stabilizers, or other structural additions. Nor is the design violently precise, for the kite can be made from either a square or an oblong piece of paper, from about 8 by 8 inches on up. The proportion of width to length should not exceed 4 to 3, but square is optimum.

The kite requires one center fold. If your paper is rectangular, begin folding so that the short sides meet, but take care to crease the paper for only a bit more than half the distance. With that fold as the basic keel, bend down (don't crease) the two front corners of the sheet so that they meet outside the fold, at the keel, about an inch back from the nose. Line them up neatly and staple them to and through the keel.

Next, mark a spot on the keel about a half inch forward of the midpoint. Put a second staple there so that it is half in and half out of the paper. The exposed prong of the staple becomes the attachment point for your flying line, the thread. Smooth out the aft section of the central fold, open up the curled-over folds up front, attach your thread, and take off.

This kite, you'll find, adapts well to most reasonable breezes. It has a remarkably level stance in the air and pulls very gently, mostly while climbing. In gusty winds, it is naturally a skitterbug; in moderate 5–10 mph air it is generally well behaved.

Another thing. This paper kite requires no tail, whereas most others need considerable lengths of it. Some, indeed, are practically paper Cobras (p. 74) and are almost entirely tail. The easiest way to make tails for paper kites is to slice a two-inch-wide roll of crepe paper into half-inch strips.

There is no end to the variety of paper kites, and experiment is so easy. There are miniature sleds, and Deltas, and all sorts of variations on the theme of paper darts. You name it, you make it, you fly it—and you'll have fun.

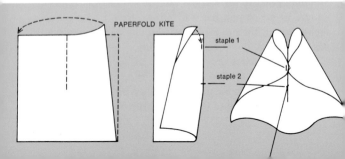

PAPERFOLD KITE

staple 1

staple 2

# THE PARAWING

Parawings, patented by Francis M. Rogallo, are distantly related, as the name suggests, to parachutes. Rogallo originally called them flexikites. Parawing is more descriptive. By any name, however, these little rigs are sturdy, almost indestructible fliers. They adapt to a wide variety of winds because there is so little about them to get out of shape. The only thing that is not free to flop is the central keel or crease. If the keel becomes crumpled or inverted, the flight is ended.

A parawing flies quite flat on the breeze, it pulls lightly, and it is not acutely sensitive to line control. But a parawing flies and is a joyful spectacle against the sky. This is another instance of a kite design that resists variation and enlargement.

The true parawing (or flexikite) measures only 15 to 20 inches square. The suggested material is Mylar, a medium-heavy plastic sheeting that may be had clear or with one side silvered. Whatever material you use, the first consideration is that the central crease or keel should hold its shape. To assure its permanence, iron in the crease. (Put a piece of paper between the material and the hot iron.) It is important, too, that the material be firm enough so that the knotted shroud lines will not pull through. The tail, or drogue, of the parawing must not be treated casually, for it is a critical part of the design.

Everything about the parawing is highly critical. In making your first parawing, follow the directions slavishly. Postpone ad-libbing until you have conquered the basic design, for the parawing is not easy.

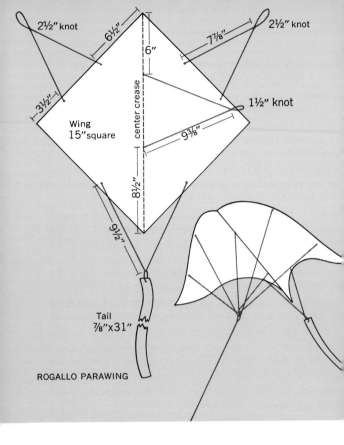

2½" knot    6½"    7⅛"    2½" knot

6"

3½"

Wing
15" square

center crease

1½" knot

9⅜"

8½"

9½"

Tail
⅞"×31"

ROGALLO PARAWING

Both the shrouds that constitute the bridle and the flying line can be monofilament or braided line in the 5- to 10-pound breaking strength bracket. But note that even the shroud knots are dimensioned accurately. The flying line attaches to the shrouds, of course, at the point where the three looped shrouds meet. When you first set up a parawing, it looks like nothing reasonable, and your first efforts to fly it may confirm your conviction that somebody made a mistake. But stay with it. The parawing may become your favorite kite because it adapts to so many kinds of weather and wind, rolling nonchalantly with the gusts.

The parawing is a light flier, with relatively little drag and not very much lift. Normally, it flies with its long, pointy nose up about 15 degrees, seldom does it tend to swim to the zenith or head for higher altitudes. Partly because it is so flexible, the parawing is not responsive to subtle control.

You may have seen articles about motorized, man-carrying versions of the parawing. Work has been done, too, toward utilizing a glider of this design to bring astronauts back to earth.

With power added, parawing kites have been used to fly manned vehicles.

This is the shape of an airfoil, the "secret" of the Jalbert design.

## THE PARAFOIL

Perhaps the most exciting of the new developments in kite design is the parafoil. Like the parawing, it has some parachute characteristics, but, more important, the parafoil is an airfoil, the shape of an airplane wing.

The story goes that Domina Jalbert, a Florida aeronautical engineer, got the idea for this kite while flying his own plane one evening. On landing, he took measurements of the cross section of his plane's wing and then designed a kite made up of half a dozen joined cells or compartments with that same shape. The cells had no structural or stiffening members. They consisted totally of sewn fabric.

Jalbert's only variation from true airfoil design was in leaving the blunt leading edge wide open so that the wind could get inside to fill out the shape. At the trailing edge he left a few small slots so that, theoretically, there might be a bit of ram-jet action. Beneath the wing he attached a series of triangular cloth vanes to provide lateral stability and to keep the kite headed into the wind. Long shrouds connected the ends of the vanes to the flying line.

The theory was that as the kite, held up facing the breeze, filled with air it became an airfoil and acquired lift from the wind flowing over and under it. Suitably

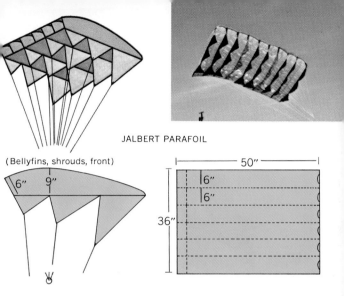

JALBERT PARAFOIL

(Bellyfins, shrouds, front)

6"   9"

50"

6"

6"

36"

controlled by the flying line, the kite should take off. After a lot of experimentation, Jalbert made his theory work. Today he is making a variety of big, specialized kites for which the government has found important use.

In the air, a three-by-four-foot parafoil looks like a floating air mattress, but it flies. The take-off is usually at the angle of a steep stall, but as it gains altitude, the kite flattens down to a more nearly normal angle of attack. The lift is remarkable. Instead of a tail, Jalbert uses a short cloth sleeve as a drogue. In medium winds, however, the drogue is not needed.

The parafoil kite is patented, and its dimensions and proportions are critical. It unites the ancient art of the kite with the very modern science of aerodynamics. It makes the wind do double duty. First it fills the wing, and then lofts it.

87

## THE DELTA-WING KITES

The delta wing is the fourth of the modern innovations in kite design. Commercially, it seems to be the most successful. Several versions of it, each duly patented, are produced and sold in large quantities. They can be rolled up for easy packaging. They can be made of either plastic sheeting or a variety of cloths. They can be decorated wildly—and they fly.

A delta wing is triangular, like the Greek letter delta ($\Delta$). The apex of the triangle is the nose, and the base is the trailing edge. The perpendicular that bisects the base is the center pole or keel. Essentially, a delta wing is a triangle of cloth or plastic in which stiffeners or battens of wood or plastic are incorporated. These stiffeners form the keel and reinforce

the leading edges of the outspread wings. In addition, there is usually an exterior spar or strut that spreads across the back of the wing (roughly halfway back) and fits into connectors on the outer edges. The purpose of this spar is to keep the wing spread open. Below the keel, a triangular vane provides directional stability. A grommet for attaching the flying line is located at the bottom of the vane.

Because the battens or stiffeners are not mechanically joined, the kite is not rigid. It moves in flight. You can see its shoulders shift as gusts come along. This gives the kite a charming, lifelike quality. The wing material, especially in the larger deltas, is brilliantly printed cloth. The total effect is spectacular. Incidentally, the larger these kites get the more they seem to tolerate coarsely woven, cloth wing covering.

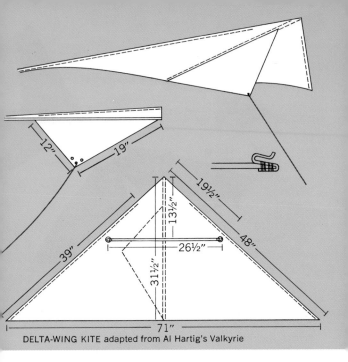

DELTA-WING KITE adapted from Al Hartig's Valkyrie

Delta-wing kites generally fly flat—on the wind rather than against. Accordingly, they do not pull as hard as you might expect.

Some kites on the market are not, strictly speaking, delta-wing kites but resemble them in general structural scheme. Some are created in the shape of hawks or fighter planes, but such concepts are really not appropriate, for the deltas are not aggressive; they are, rather, graceful floaters. In some variants, the nose of the "V" is flattened so that the airborne shape is trapezoidal. Incidentally, because the covering should not be taut, plastic sheeting (bagging) can be used.

# ASSORTED KITES

For every kite so far described there are dozens of variations. There is simply no limit to what can be done with paper, cloth, plastic, a few sticks, and a vivid imagination. Several of the schools of design and technology hold annual competitions for novel, fantastic, far-out kite designs. Some of them actually fly. Others are strictly aesthetic. Because they are composed of planes and triangles and circles they look like kites, but that's all. A few kites, produced commercially, might give you an idea or two in making your own design. You'll soon improve on any design.

## Revolving Wings

Under the trade name of Rotoki, a kite is sold that consists of airfoils curled up within a cylinder or cylinders. In a steady breeze, the cylinders whirl rapidly on a horizontal axis, and as they whirl, they develop lift. The whole contraption then sails off.

A toy-like variant of the revolving-wing kite.

Towed into a light wind, the Bensen Gyroglider
becomes a man-carrying kite.

Revolving wing kites never fly very high nor at a
high angle. Aerodynamically, these kites are real
curiosities. They are made of molded plastic or of a
metallic paper, so few of us are equipped to build such
kites at home.

Another form of rotating-wing kite utilizes the autogyro principle. Free-wheeling horizontal rotors spin
on vertical axes. Lift is developed—and up they go.
During World War II, German submarines carried autogyro kites big enough to lift a man. Well out to sea, a
surfaced submarine would tow such a kite, with an
observer aboard, to considerable altitudes, from which
the horizon was scanned for enemy patrols or ships.
By phone, the spotter kept the deck informed of what
he saw. If he was unlucky enough to spot a nearby
destroyer or plane, he was unceremoniously cut loose
as the sub dove for safety.

Autogyros are not helicopters, though both use long,

thin rotors that are actually airfoils. In an autogyro the rotors are not power driven. After an assisted start, they revolve by wind power. And unlike helicopter blades, they are flexibly mounted so that the lift developed by an advancing blade is not .canceled by a retreating blade.

Free-wheeling model airplane propellers or spinners are often mounted on otherwise conventional kites. They whirl and buzz, but signify very little.

If you become interested in trying an autogyro kite, do not be discouraged. The autogyro principle is tricky, with more imponderables than the income tax.

Dr. Bell once concocted a circular biplane kite about ten feet in diameter. It flew, after a fashion, but it lacked the stability of his beloved tetrahedrals. Others have put together kites of incredibly complex design but complexity, it seems, doesn't necessarily spell success in kiting. The great kites—kites such as the Eddy, the Indian fighter kites, the Conyne, the Scott, and the other modern, flexible designs—are all simple.

Alexander Graham Bell's circular or ring kite.

## Airplane Kites

"Airplane" kites are generally simply conventional Eddy-type kites with clear plastic wing covering on which is printed, more or less realistically, the semblance of an airplane. They are not airplane kites at all. To produce a true airplane kite takes a lot of work and a fistful of skill. Here's why.

One of the essentials of a kite is drag, a combination of forces set up by gravity, the kite line, and the push of the wind on the face of the kite. When a kite manages to develop enough lift to rise above the backward push of drag, it climbs. But even as it climbs, drag is still operative. It serves, in fact, to help keep the kite stable.

When you deliberately design a kite to fly as an airplane flies, you are asking for trouble, for a good airplane has relatively little drag, the less the better.

A delta-wing kite with an airplane design printed on its clear, plastic surface.

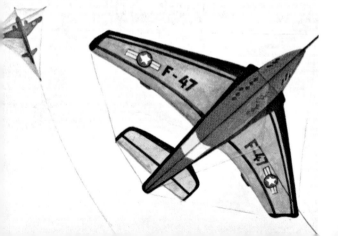

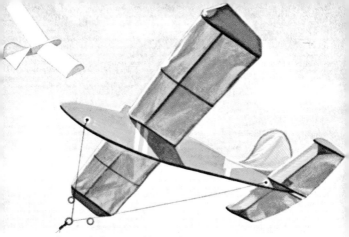

A true airplane-type kite needs strong, steady wind.

It gets most of its lift from the quickened flow of air above its main airfoil. Its efficiency increases as drag is eliminated. When you build an airplane and try to fly it in kite fashion, you have an anachronism. As a glider it may be fine, but on a tow line, it tends to swim right up overhead. At that point it "red lines." Catastrophe beckons.

What your glider-kite really needs is drag. You can get drag by increasing the angle of incidence or attack of the main wing, or you can change the bridling so that the whole thing is canted upward in a kind of permanent stall. A third possibility is to incorporate "spoilers" in the wing, just as is done to give soaring planes or airliners aerial brakes.

Soaring kites, similar to unpowered gliders, have been made and flown. They have to be built with great care and flown on light monofilament lines. Like airplane kites, they behave well under perfect conditions.

### NOISY KITES

According to legend, some of antiquity's most famous kites carried noisemakers. The noises were intended to inspire, frighten, mystify, or simply amuse the people over whom the kites were flown.

A stretched, wide rubber band held edge-on to the wind sets up vibrations that cannot only be heard but are almost musical. Such a hummer can be added to any rigid-frame kite. A strip of cloth or paper about an inch wide stretched between two struts is the simplest. If you have a folding, nonrigid kite, you will have to suspend a frame of some sort from the kite line, just below the kite. A triangle, the kind shown, p. 106, works for just about any kind of noisemaker—a bamboo pipe, a bell, or whatever may appeal to you.

Incidentally, a braided kite line sets up a very fine whistle when the wind is good and your kite is pulling

The simplest of all hummers is a strip of very light paper, pasted over a taut line between two extended longerons.

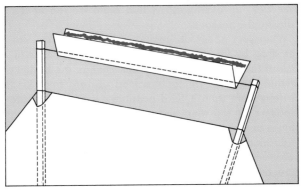

Firecrackers, attached to a kite's tail, do not interfere with its flying qualities.

well. You can get a musical note from that tensed line by plucking it. The pitch rises with the pull.

The Chinese are historically famous for firecrackers and have been setting them off from kites for ages. The trick is to delay ignition until the kite is well up. This is done with either a long fuse or by using a stick of punk that does not ignite the firecracker for five minutes or so. This is good fun, but do not try it where fire hazards exist or where firecrackers are prohibited by law.

Lighted kites are also legendary. Japanese lanterns or small battery-powered flashlights can be put aloft with only one difficulty: in ordinary weather, the wind tends to drop at sundown, when your light would begin to be visible.

# KITE-LINE CLIMBERS

When your kite is up and flying serenely, the temptation usually arises to send something else up on that long, slender line. Every kiteflying boy has certainly sent up "messages"—simply square or round sheets of paper torn so that the center of the sheet engages the flying line. The tear is covered with a bit of adhesive tape to keep it from falling off. Dozens of such messages can go aloft on a single line. Add a curl to the messenger's corners, and it will spin as it climbs.

The simplest commercial variation on this theme is made of plastic and wire, with loops to slide along the kite line. It is pulled up the line by a small plastic parachute that opens into the breeze. When its front hits a cork, thoughtfully anchored on the line before flying, a sliding wire is pushed back, thereby freeing the parachute which begins its descent.

After parachutes, the most favored drop loads are paper or balsa gliders. Unless you are very lucky, of course, even a ten-cent glider dropped from a thousand feet up can manage to land inconveniently far from your flying pad. Think twice before sending up a carefully made glider on which you have labored long.

Some kite men send up bags of flour which, on release, "explode" satisfyingly into a little cloud. The same happens with bags of confetti. You can also send up a dozen or two strips of light paper and watch them whirl and dance before they finally settle to the ground.

Kite-line gadgetry: (1) the classic "messenger," a square of paper; (2) a paper pinwheel centered on the flying line; (3) a simple burning-punk release device for gliders; (4) a paper straw, slit and rejoined around the flying lines, which can also be fitted with sails to make it climb; (5) a bundle of thin paper slices, released by #6 device from far up to whirl and soar for many minutes; (6) a simple version of the bumper-drop mechanism shown in a more elaborate version on p. 100.

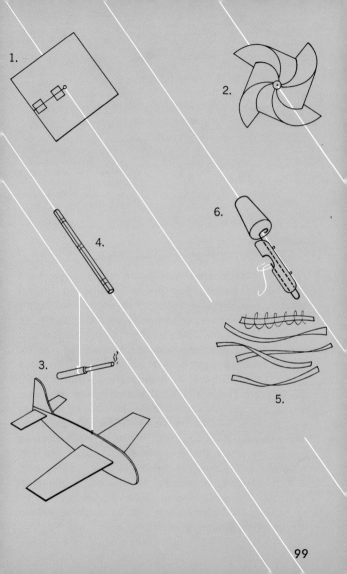

1.

2.

4.

6.

3.

5.

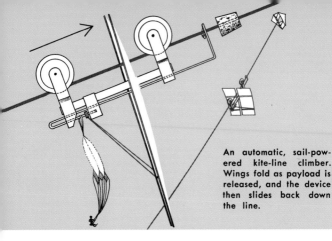

An automatic, sail-powered kite-line climber. Wings fold as payload is released, and the device then slides back down the line.

More sophisticated kite-line climbers have been evolved, of course. Ray Biehler, the kiting physics teacher, has made a beauty that sports two deeply grooved aluminum wheels or pulleys which ride the flying line. A "feeler" on the front of the climber hits a cork on the line, and then a thin wire rod, the far end of which is bent back to slide through the drop gates, is pushed back. As it slides, two separate gates are opened. The first releases the pay load, whatever it may be, and the second frees the sails so that they are no longer held flat to the wind. The sails thereupon fold inward, and deprived of its kite-line-climbing power, the whole shebang slides back down the line. A small cushion or mitt is needed to stop it at the end.

It is possible, of course, to operate drops electronically. The same kind of radio impulse that is used by radio-control plane pilots can be made to work a dropping mechanism on a kite.

# KITE PHOTOGRAPHY

The idea of hoisting a camera by kite for the purposes of aerial photography is far from new. George Eastman, the Kodak man, worked on this idea back in the 1890's. Sundry others experimented with it at about the same time, all hoping to achieve what were then called "bird's-eye views" of the landscape.

Eastman's classic aerial view of Kodak Park, 1907, was made with a small, lightweight camera loaded with flexible film. The camera was lifted some 500 feet by a kite about six feet tall. The trick, then as now, was to control the instant of exposure. With a really big kite

George Eastman was one of the first industrialists to get a "bird's eye view" of his plant with a kite-lofted camera. This is Kodak Park, Rochester, as of 1907.

The devastation of San Francisco after the earthquake-fire of 1906 was vividly pictured with a big panoramic camera carried high by a train of seventeen enormous kites. The flying line was a heavy rope handled by a team of husky men. George Lawrence, the photographer, used binoculars to determine that the camera was aimed right before he triggered the shutter by means of a wired electrical impulse.

it is easily possible to use a separate line, the sole function of which is to trigger the shutter.

If the camera is fastened to the kite itself or to a platform affixed to the line just below the kite, some sort of delayed-action shutter release must be contrived. The time-honored solution is a length of punk or burning string. The fire eats its way along the punk (or whatever) until it encounters a crossing thread that is connected under tension to the camera shutter. When the thread is burned through the tension is broken, and the shutter snaps.

An exposure so made is obviously a willy-nilly thing. If the angle and the orientation of the shot are right,

you get a useful picture. But you have no real control.

Similarly, there is very little control with a system that utilizes a kite-line climber. The climber, with luck, struggles up the line, carrying a small camera, all loaded and set. When the climber nudges the stop on the line, a trigger is released, and a picture made. But you have no way of determining exactly which way the camera will be pointed at the instant of exposure. You can get box cameras for as little as a dollar, so your loss will not be great if your rig gets bashed.

Kite photography is fascinating, but it is by no means easy. You need good wind, good light, and proper functioning of several bits of "machinery."

# TRAINS

The idea of flying more than one kite from a single line is usually associated with weight-lifting projects. But even when you have no such job to do, the spectacle of several kites operating far up on the line in your hand (or on your reel, preferably) is rewarding.

A few rules are involved. Common sense suggests that the first kite up should be a reliable, level-headed performer, for it is the "anchor man" of the formation. After it is securely in the air, launch the second kite. With kite A up, say, a hundred yards and kite B up fifty, cut and attach B's line to A's line—and continue to pay out A's line.

As you do so, watch kite B's behavior. If it flies at a lower angle than kite A, there's a good chance that it can foul the main line. Obviously, therefore, you can set up a working rule that the flying angles of the kites which comprise the train should be about the same. A second rule will suggest itself; keep the several kites well apart in distance up the line.

One "train" kiter has reported a delightful maneuver. He gets half a dozen similar kites up, all serenely flying in formation, then suddenly lets the formation have about twenty yards of slack. The kites thereupon put on a wild show. Each kite darts, dodges, dives, and cavorts until the slack is used up. Then they slide back into formation.

All sorts of stories about "record" numbers of kites being flown *en train* have been circulated. They range from twenty to a hundred. For most of us, the spectacle of even half a dozen kites deploying from a single line is amply satisfying. Handling a covey of capricious kites can become more than an ordinary handful.

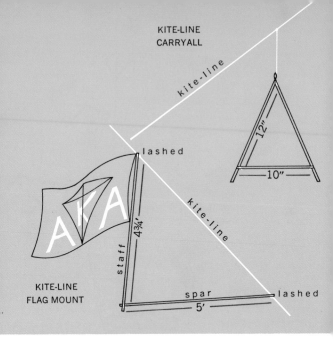

KITE-LINE
CARRYALL

kite-line

12"

10"

lashed

kite-line

A K A

4¾'

staff

KITE-LINE
FLAG MOUNT

spar

lashed

5'

## FLAGS

Flags fly most spectacularly from kite lines. While a flag or pennant can be tied directly to the flying line, you get better display of a big flag by holding it away from the line with a short yardarm attached to the lower end of the kite's halyard.

If you are flying your nation's flag, be careful lest it be dropped unceremoniously, snagged by trees, or dragged across the ground.

The kite-line carryall is simply a light wooden triangle attached to the flying line.

# FISHING

There are two schools of thought about using kites to help catch fish. One assumes a relatively short fish line attached firmly part way up the kite's flying line. The other uses a full-length fishing line which is held to the flying line with a pinch-type clothespin. A striking fish yanks the line free, and thereafter fish and kite are played separately. This is the method used by a number of sailfishermen in Florida waters. Usually, they purchase a complete rig which includes a square-diamond kite, a big mahogany reel, a socket to hold it to the side of the boat, and plenty of 60-pound dacron line. The cost is about $50 per outfit. Two or more fishing lines can be pinned to one kite line.

Both styles of kite fishing capitalize on the fact that a kite-suspended fish line can be far out, away from the boat or shore; both require steady, hard-pulling, low-angle kites, usually cloth-covered.

A "skiter" at Cypress Gardens, Florida.

## WATER-SKI KITING

A relatively recent addition to water-ski competitions and spectacles is water-ski kiting, or skiting. It is wonderful to watch but is quite a specialized sport. The kites are usually large, two-masted variants of the Eddy format with aluminum frames. There are slings in which the skiers "sit," plus bars to cling to. The major factor in the kite's flight, of course, is the speed of the towing boat and the wind. The skier controls the angle of incidence of his kite, and, accordingly, his take-offs and landings. By moving his arms and body, he has some lateral control, but these controls are within fairly narrow limits.

# TOWED KITES

The military of several countries have used towed kites to train anti-aircraft gunners. These kite targets, usually Eddy-shaped, may be about seven feet high. On the broad surface the outline of a fighter plane may be painted. Towed by a jeep such a kite gives gun crews a lot to shoot at, but the altitude and apparent speed of such a target far from match the real thing.

Towed kites used during World War II as improvements over the barrage-balloon technique were really effective. They were big 20-foot Hargrave-type box kites, flown on wire lines from the decks of convoy ships. Their prime purpose was to ward off dive bombers attempting to bomb or to strafe merchant ships. No pilot relished the idea of fouling his propeller in the almost invisible wire kite lines. The kites were relatively expendable. Harry Sauls, of Miami Beach, was the man who developed them.

Harry Sauls and one of his smaller barrage kites.

## KITE CONTESTS AND FLY-INS

Get two or more kite fliers together—and you have a competition on your hands. Make up the rules as you go along.

If you are involved with youngsters—Boy Scouts, Boys' Clubs, and such—you will need to set up a series of classes and events, in order to keep things from getting out of hand. Categories such as these might be established:

1. Homemade kites: with special awards for ingenuity, design, workmanship, and performance.
2. Purchased kites, tailed: with awards for altitude, angle, duration, and control.
3. Purchased kites, tailless: awards similar to above.

A typical fly-in brings out kites in fantastic variety.

4. Kitemanship: with prizes for maneuvering, fast climbing, etc.; greatest altitude reached in five minutes is a standard judging factor.

5. Kite duels: between matched pairs, to see who can knock the other out of the air by direct contact. If paired contestants are equipped to fight in the Indian fashion, with either abrasives or small knives on their lines, fine!

6. Bomb dropping: contestants who have release gadgets could compete for accuracy, dropping small sacks of flour on targets.

Organizers of such events will undoubtedly work out a point system so that a winner and a runner-up can be determined. In any event, give extra points for non-running launches and for controlled landings.

111

Fifty years ago mobs of boys gathered whenever kites flew. They're still doing it.

To avoid disgruntled contestants and disputed decisions, use as many specific, impersonal measuring devices as possible. Fast-climbing competitions, for examples, should be judged on the basis of measured lengths of line and the time taken to get them all up. Measure the pull of kites with a good spring scale. The "smallest" and "largest" kites can be measured with yardsticks or tapes. And a simple wind meter will give you the answer to the question, Whose kite flies in the lightest breeze?

The usual fly-in procedure is to have the contestants work in pairs or teams. Thus, simultaneous launchings can be achieved, with one boy holding the kite while his teammate handles the line.

Because it is seldom possible to fly from your own yard, within easy reach of your workbench and repair-replacement supplies, it is a good thing to make up an easily portable kit of the most-needed items.

First, a few tools: sharp-nosed pliers, a couple of good knives, a folding ruler, scissors, and maybe an eyeleter for improvising new bridle points.

Replacement or repair materials must be tailored to the kites you fly. Include a swatch of covering material, splints for repairing spars, a supply of swivel snaps, cord for wing hems, and extra rings and flying line.

Take a tube of fast-working cement, a roll of pressure-sensitive tape, and needle and thread.

Your wind-velocity meter should be in the kit, along with any other available instruments (range finders, height finders, etc.), and a pair of binoculars. (It is surprising how often a closeup look is helpful.) Finally, don't forget a pair of supple leather gloves.

All of these items will fit easily in a small case.

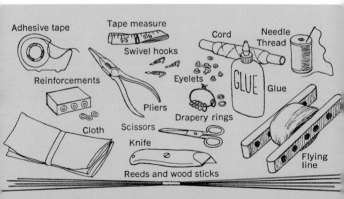

# KITES, KITE SUPPLIES, AND ACCESSORIES

Kiting is still a refreshingly unorganized business. Most of the dozen or so kite manufacturers are small; some of those listed here may have vanished between list-making and publication.

## WHERE TO GET KITES

In recent years scores of new kite shops have sprung up, mostly in resort areas. They are good sources because they are usually run by people who know something about kites and offer a variety of models, plus accessories. Hobby and sport shops sometimes carry kites; if they also carry fishing line, reels, etc., so much the better. Supermarket paper or plastic kites are generally the least sophisticated.

The best known "general store" of kiting is the **Go Fly a Kite Shop**, 1434 Third Avenue, New York, N.Y. 10028. An illustrated price list is available; much of their business is by mail. Mrs. Surhendra Bahadur is the proprietor.

**Come Fly a Kite** in San Francisco's Ghirardelli Square is the biggest, brightest, liveliest kitery I know. Dinesh Bahadur is the dynamic spark plug. All sorts of kites, well displayed.

**The Kite Factory**, Box 9081, Seattle, Wash. 98109, specializes in well-made, high-performance kites, including parafoils, deltas, Gruvel Bullets, and special sleds. Dave Checkley sells direct as well as through selected retailers.

---

## KITE MAKERS

**Ace-Hi Company**, P.O. Box 188, Gracie Station, N.Y.C. 10028. Makes inexpensive, paper covered, bowed two-stickers.

**Alan-Whitney Company**, P.O. Box 447, New Haven, Conn., Harold Levine, manager, makes the Space Bird kite. About $5.

**Airplane Kite Company**, 1702 W. Third, Roswell, New Mexico, produces the airplane-like Blackhawk Kites, a Skyscraper, and the Kittyhawk. Priced from $2.35 to $3.50. Ray Holland is the manager.

**Crunden Martin Mfg. Company**, 760 S. Second, St. Louis, Mo. Box kite specialists.

**Gayla Industries**, 4326 Pinemont (P.O. Box 10800), Houston, Texas, Les Phillips, president. Probably the world's largest producer of kites in the $1 to $4 range, all plastic-covered and colorful. Found in most hobby, sport, and specialty shops.

**Hartig Kites,** Box 1356, Nantucket, Mass., Al Hartig, proprietor. Excellent Delta-wing kites. The Ace is smallish; the Valkyrie has a wing span of about five feet. Flight tested, well made. Al Hartig's are the most beautiful of high-quality kites. Fly well in moderate winds. Priced from $10 up.

**Hi-Flier Kites,** 510 E. Wabash, Decatur, Ill., John Winick, president. Very inexpensive paper-covered two-stickers and box kites for the supermarket and toy-shop trade.

**Lewis Products Company,** P.O. Box 982, Kendall, Fla. Kite-fishing outfits, including a square kite, rod, mahogany reel, hardware, and 60-lb. dacron line at $49.50.

**Mots Kites,** 3141 W. Juneau Ave., Milwaukee, Wisc. Frank Mots deals only in his own "acrobatic" kites.

**North Pacific Products,** 1224 E. Second Ave., Bend, Ore., R. W. Mair, sales manager. Producers of the Glite, a combination glider and kite.

**Skyway Products,** 1104 Pacific, Brooklyn, N.Y. Specializes in the Rocket, a plastic version of the Eddy kite.

**Striegel Mfg. Company,** 1223 Arcade Ave., Louisville, Ky. Produces the Superkite, a version of the triangular box.

---

## LINE SOURCES

Check your hardware stores for mason's twine. It is usually twisted or braided nylon and made in a variety of weights and strengths. Most stores carry only #18, which is a bit on the heavy side; #15 or #12 are best for most average-sized kites.

Seine twine, a marine supply item, comes in one-pound skeins. Number 6 comes 3,300 feet to the pound-skein; its breaking strength is 10 lbs. Number 9, 2,150 feet per pound, has a breaking strength of 18 lbs. Number 12, 1,600 feet to the skein, rates 24 lbs. in breaking strength.

Bonded filament, from the **K. T. Netcraft Co.,** 3101 Sylvania Ave., Toledo, Ohio 43613, is another marine line. The number 3 grade comes 8,300 feet to the skein, with a breaking strength of 20. Number 5 runs 4,800 feet to the pound, with a breaking strength of 38. The heavier grades get pesky to handle.

Monofilament, a DuPont product, is available through Netcraft (above). Cheap but cranky. Almost invisible in the air. Under strong pull, can cut and slash dangerously; use with care.

Braided nylon line is supplied by the **Riverside Products Co.,** P.O. Box 335, Riverside, Ill. 60546.

For lighter kites, the button thread used by tailors (No. 16, 4 cord) is perfectly good. It comes in 500-yard spools.

**Cloth.** Lightweight (1.5 oz. or less), rip-stop woven nylon is excellent. Used primarily for sailboat spinnakers, this cloth is a marina item. Or it can be mailordered from suppliers to sailmakers; one such—and very obliging—is Howe & Bainbridge, Inc., 220 Commercial St., Boston, Mass. 02109. Ask for rip-stop kite cloth. In many colors, from rolls 38" wide. Not cheap.

Some fabric shops carry a lining material called Nylon Parchment, which is kite-worthy. Tightly woven, lightweight cotton prints (the gaudier the better) are fine for larger kites. Beware of slick, slidey stuff; it is hard to handle and to sew.

**Paper.** A synthetic paper called Tyvek is made by DuPont and sold through larger paper dealers; it is very tough, works easily, and takes color well. The lighter weights of Type 10 are kite-suitable; the softer, minutely perforated Type 16 is marginal. Some dealers offer it in large sheets; others will cut yardages from 56" rolls on order.

**Rice paper** (Tableau paper or cloth) is sold at most hobby shops in sheets or cut from wide rolls. Rice paper is soft and tears easily, but mends with plastic tape. Takes paste and color well. Okay for beginners.

Plain brown wrapping paper, lightweight, works well; generally available in yard-wide rolls. White shelf paper is not as good; it tears readily and gets brittle.

**Plastic** sheeting is available in great variety and color. The flexible type (used in leaf bags, drop cloths, etc.) is preferable, but watch out for excessive stretching. Special cements, staples, or controlled heat needed for joints.

## KITE ORGANIZATIONS

### ACCESSORIES

**Wind Meters** (anemometers). Least expensive and handiest, yet adequately accurate, is the Dwyer Wind Meter; most easily available from Edmund Scientific Co., Barrington, N.J. 08007, whose catalog you should have anyway. About $10. More complex and costly are the Sims Anemometer (Annapolis, Md. 21401) and the Windial by Airguide Instrument Co., 2210 Wabansia Ave., Chicago, Ill. 60647.

**Range Finders.** To use the height finder described on p. 42, distance to kite must be known. Optical range finders can be useful but beware of cheap "golfing" outfits. Ranging, Inc., 90 Lincoln Rd. N., East Rochester, N.Y. 14445, makes a good range finder for kiting at about $45. Height finders used in rocketry are not much good for kiting. Odometers or rev-counters are useful, but appropriate ones are hard to find. Veeder Root, 70 Sargeant St., New Haven, Conn. 06102, is probably the best source for such instruments.

# BOOKS

**Downer, Marion,** KITES, HOW TO MAKE AND FLY THEM, Lothrop, New York, 1959. For younger kite fliers. Many illustrations.

**Fowler, H.,** KITES, A PRACTICAL GUIDE TO KITE MAKING AND FLYING, Ronald, New York, 1953. Primarily for boys and girls.

**Hart, Clive,** KITES, AN HISTORICAL SURVEY, Frederick A. Praeger, New York, 1967. An expensive ($12.50) but beautiful and comprehensive book; the classic in this field.

**Hart, Clive,** YOUR BOOK OF KITES, Transatlantic Arts, Inc., New York, 1964. For boys, but anyone can learn from it.

**Hunt, Leslie,** KITES THAT FLY, Dover Publishing, New York.

**Jue, David F.,** CHINESE KITES, C. E. Tuttle Co., Rutland, Vt., 1967. A small but well illustrated and authentic book.

**Newman, Lee and Jay,** KITECRAFT, Crown Publishers, Inc., New York, 1975. Big, colorful, fairly up-to-date.

**Pelham, David,** KITES, The Penguin Book of, Viking-Penguin, New York, 1976. One of the best, historically and technically.

**Ridgway, Harold,** KITE MAKING AND FLYING, Grammercy Publishing New York. Good section on kite aerodynamics.

**Schulz, Charles,** GO FLY A KITE, CHARLIE BROWN, Holt, Rinehart and Winston, New York, 1960. Completely charming.

**Stemple, Jane Yolen,** THE WORLD ON A STRING, World Publ. Co., New York, 1968. Jane, daughter of famed kitesman, Will Yolen, treats the history and spirit of kite flying very well.

**Wagenvoord, James,** FLYING KITES, Macmillan, New York, 1968. A handsome book; some practical information and more on the aesthetics of kites and kite flying.

**Yolen, Will,** KITES and KITE FLYING, Simon & Schuster, New York, 1976. The old maestro tells all.

Domina Jalbert launches a big new Parafoil-Sled.

## KITE ORGANIZATIONS

Kite fliers are represented by only one national organization, the American Kitefliers Association. Unusual for such an organization, it actually resists efforts or tendencies to solemnize, glorify, or complicate itself. Bob Ingraham is editor of *Kite Tales*, the association's quarterly publication. His address, Box 1511, Silver City, N.M. 87102 is also the headquarters address. The annual membership fee is five dollars, and it is worth much more than that just to read Bob's comments and reports.

**Photo credits:** Brown Brothers, 17, 19, 112; Department of Atmospheric Science, Colorado State University, 33; Harry Sauls, 50; Bensen Aircraft, 92; Smithsonian Institution, 93; Eastman Kodak, 101; California Historical Society, San Francisco, 102-103; Cypress Gardens, 108. All other photos by Wyatt Brummitt.